The
4 Most Important
Questions
You Can Ask

The
4 Most Important Questions
You Can Ask

❖

Powerful Lessons in Personal and Professional Change

Dr. Bradford A. Seaman

To order additional copies of this book, contact:
Xlibris Corporation
1-888-795-4274
www.Xlibris.com
Orders@Xlibris.com
60274

CONTENTS

THE AUTHOR'S OVERVIEW OF THE BOOK

The 4 Most Important Questions You Can Ask

Powerful Lessons in Personal and Professional Change

Dr. Brad guides individuals as they develop answers to The 4 Key Directional Questions every person must ask as they walk the path of self-improvement toward personal and professional growth.

1. **Where are you going?**
    Know that direction is the most important factor to any strategy for long-term success. Understand that without a clear sense of direction you cannot experience lasting change or have a positive influence on the world around you.

2. **Why is going there important?**
    Knowing the "why" will push you to grow. Understand that if the why is not defined well, and is not connected to a daily discipline with a clear direction, it will not have lasting importance.

3. Who is going there with you?

Know that building the right team is essential to getting where you want to go. Understand that without the right people on the bus, seated in the right seats, and doing the right jobs with passion and a clear goal, you will not arrive at your destination.

4. How are you going to get there?

Know that a well thought-out written plan is a map essential for lasting success. Understand that a detailed plan allows for the shared knowledge of qualities and direction that lead to desired success.

Dr. Brad knows that lasting success includes balancing the 4 Keys to the Formula of Personal Achievement.

1. Develop an intellectual blueprint plan.

One's experiences are not enough to shape performance. Each individual must strive continually to broaden understanding by implementing a plan of continuous intellectual enrichment. In order to have lasting importance, you need to pursue continuous opportunities for personal and professional intellectual development.

2. Develop a Mentor—Mentoring blueprint plan for self-development.

Each person's life is enriched and strengthened by being part of good relationships. There are two parts in the formula for achieving growth through relationships. The first: plan to include people of character and integrity in your life. This is best done through mentoring roles, both personal and professional. Seek out a mentor who will continue to ask the 4 Key Direction Questions Dr. Brad has outlined for you here in this book. Make sure your mentor requires accountability in your response. The second: understand the need to be a mentor to individuals who desire to grow and benefit from others' experience and wisdom, and who will someday step into positions of leadership after having unique guidance from you.

3. **Develop a blueprint plan to guide your ethical and moral integrity in decision-making.**
The moral, spiritual, and ethical areas of our lives are vastly important to lasting balance and personal effectiveness. Understand one cannot separate or compartmentalize one's life. All actions are intertwined, so everything you do impacts all areas of your life. It is not enough to have a healthy body if you are morally ineffective. You can have lots of friends, but the wrong associations. These wrong associations will not allow you to live a life of lasting importance.

4. **Develop a blueprint plan to guide your physical health and diet.**
One's physical health is essential to one's performance. If you do not feel well, you will not perform well. Dr. Brad emphasizes the importance of balancing healthy eating, weight control, and consistent exercise. He knows this is achieved by making a reasonable promise to yourself that you will keep. He knows that when you over promise, you set yourself up for failure. This book is about the daily disciplines that lead you along the path of success and to the richness of a life well lived.

ACKNOWLEDGEMENTS

I want to acknowledge my deep appreciation to my wife Ellie for the expressions of her love and adoration of me. In all my life, I have never had someone as sincerely grateful and admiring of me as she has been. I cannot mention to you how many times I've stood in awe of her joyous spirit and the expression of genuine love she shows. She is truly a jewel. I am fortunate to have her in my life. She is my best friend and greatest cheerleader. She is also practical and grounded, which helps me remain focused. Above all, I adore her genuine, sincere spirit. She challenges me in my own walk to want to be a better person.

I want to thank Karen Allen for all of the countless hours of reading, re-reading, and editing she has done for me to get this book ready for publication. She is highly skilled in spelling and grammar, something I struggle with as a writer wanting to be heard but not embarrassed. This book has become a labor of love for the both of us. I truly could not have gotten this far without her skills and support. So a deep thanks to you Karen. You are a blessing beyond my ability to thank you.

I want to take the time to thank Marybeth Kingsley for all the hours she has spent reading behind Karen and me. Her extra set of eyes have help place the book into a practical format to help it be easily read and applicable to those who will use it as a tool to enrich their lives. So a deep thanks to you Marybeth. You have enriched my life and will others because of your untiring dedication.

I want to take the time to thank all those who have struggled to find their way in this world. The struggles to learn how to make life better that have touch my life have found their ways into books, lectures, and training, enriching me with a wealth of knowledge to share with others seeking better lives {or something along those lines}. I am deeply grateful and indebted to you. There are too many of you to mention, but the Great Record Keeper knows. He is the one whose voice matters the most.

I want to thank all my friends who have allowed me to talk my way through this writing process. You have supported me, encouraged me, and added your own sets of insights to my attempt to be heard. You have helped make this happen. You truly are jewels in the Crown of Life.

I want to take the time to thank my clients who have opened their lives to me. You have shared you deepest fears, wants, and the secrets of your lives. I count that the most enriching expression of the true human spirit. Your honesty has opened up opportunities for both of us to learn what only honesty and truth can teach. I am a better human being for your willingness to embrace the opportunity to change. You are a fresh breath of air in a world struggling to find meaning and purpose.

Finally, I want to thank my parents, Gene and Gerry, who taught me the importance of living a life well lived. In their human frailty, they planted in my heart as an 11-year-old child one thing of lasting importance that remains strong within me today as a present, ever influencing prize beyond all value. A deep thanks to you for planting that tiny seed of faith and nurturing it throughout my childhood, adolescence, and throughout my adult life.

Thank you to those of you who pick up this book and read it. I entrust to you this road map to a life of meaning and purpose. May your journey be as well lived as the life you seek. May you be so enriched that you cannot begin to express your stories of success.

Dr. Brad

INTRODUCTION

What Are the 4 Most Important Questions You Can Ask?

We all hope to live a fantastic, full life. Often our realities can seem so far away from our wishes, hopes, dreams, and intentions. The gathering of this material comes from many places. My purpose is to help you find a crucial, central point for your life so *you* can find and create a life well lived. Despite what you might think, this book is not really a self-help book. It is about learning the 4 Most Important Questions of how to be extraordinary as a means to achieving what is most important to you.

I believe that these 4 Most Important Questions open the path to living life to its fullest. I believe that searching to become extraordinary moves you from settling for a good life to experiencing a fantastic one. I believe this book is about achieving passion and purpose in your life at its core.

To achieve this crucial point of being incredible, every individual must answer these 4 Most Important Questions:

The *first* most important question you can ask yourself is:

Where am I going?

15

The _second_ most important question you can ask yourself is:

Why is going there so important to me?

The _third_ most important question you can ask yourself is:

Who is going on the journey with me?

The _fourth_ and final most important question you must ask yourselves is:

How am I going to get there?

The Timeless Principles of _Direction_ and _Purpose._

Before you spend a lot of time answering these questions, let me tell you a story that has greatly influenced my thinking. I was in the Army for 14 years, and my first assignment as an officer was with an artillery unit. Within this unit there is a person called a Forward Observer. The job of the Forward Observer in combat is to be close enough to the target to call in a mortar round on it. I quickly found out the importance of being close enough to see the target, yet far enough away not to _be_ the target. Under the fire of combat, you cannot afford to be careless in your thinking and execution while calling in a mortar round. Nope! Such a decision would become a huge problem for you in just a matter of seconds. Think about it! Being careless here would wreck your whole day. Here is where I discovered that _direction and purpose were the most important rules for guiding decision making._ This story shows how crucial they are.

This experience showed me the value of these 4 Most Important Questions that comprise the timeless principles of direction. They are the primary governing factors to your life, career, and everything else you will encounter in building an incredible life.

I also learned in map reading class that if you did not apply these 4 Most Important Questions, you could walk around lost for days. You might even die while being close to people and not know it.

The same 4 Most Important Questions became essential in being trained to use a compass. I learned the importance of true north on the compass. I learned that magnetic north is a principle that is always present whether you are paying attention to it or not. I learned that the compass did not need light to work. It worked fine even in the dark. I also learned that the compass did not need land to work. It worked in the open sea, even when land was days away. With that knowledge, I learned to trust the compass to give me clear direction when the way seemed unclear and I was uncertain. I learned that north does not change, regardless of circumstances.

You, too, you have a *True North* stamped inside of you. True North represents the sum of all the principles and laws that govern everything you do, from building strong relationships, to being integrity centered, to achieving financial freedom. Oh sure, you can decide not to pay attention to these principles and laws that govern living. You have this freedom of choice. However, I learned that ignoring them results in being lost, frustrated, and feeling like a failure. Who needs that?

If your find yourself broke and confused, this book is for you.

If your relationships have failed, this book is for you.

If you are deadlocked in your career, this book is for you.

If you can ask yourself the hard question such as, "Why isn't my life turning out the way I feel it should for me?" this book is for you.

This book is designed to help you find lasting importance.

With these questions and the words on the pages of this book, I trust that you will see how adjusting your life map and flawed thinking will serve you well. These True North Life Principles will help you set your direction toward getting all those things that are truly valuable and important to you. It is realizing that your thinking, which shapes the maps you use to guide your life, has gotten you to where you are right now, with what you have right now. If you do not feel like life has given you what you want, *you have the power to change it! You do this by answering these 4 Most Important Questions for yourself.*

Now you can begin to adjust your direction by living your life centered on these 4 Most Important Questions. They represent the True North Life Principles and Laws that govern all of life and living.

Adjusting your old ways of thinking and behaving tunes you into the internal passion that draws you along, achieving truly amazing things. I believe you will have a stamp upon your life that gives you a unique passion. You will have a unique set of skills and talents that accompany you, helping you achieve incredible success for yourself. You will attract those things to yourself that will give you lasting importance. These sets of skills, coupled with this unique passion, significantly influence the larger community around you. Living an extraordinary life with true joy comes to those who keep asking themselves these 4 Most Important Questions. These questions influence ordinary actions and bring about amazing achievements.

So how do you begin this exceptional new life?

First, admit that you are not achieving the things that are valuable and important to you. Stop fueling your frustration by continuing to follow the thinking that has gotten you what you now have. Admitting this helps determine how to get to where you want to be. Once you admit this, then you can make the proper corrections and move on. Coming to this realization will help you step onto the path toward gaining an astonishing life for yourself. This admission is the first step to creating a life map to steer you *from an ordinary life to a fantastic one.* This new map will help guide you away from your old destination and toward a new one. It will help you make the life changing corrections you need to find *a life filled with passion and purpose.* Is it simple? No! Is it going to be worth it in the end? Yes!

I invite you to participate!

This book's design is to guide you through a testing of the maps and rules you now use to govern your decisions. Until you come to this turning point, you cannot pinpoint flaws in your direction and execution. Once you admit you are lost, frustrated, and not getting the things you want, then you can make adjustments and choose a new direction. *Knowing where you want to go is the first important question you can ask yourself when charting your new course.* It establishes your new map and governs all other activities.

Thus, this book is about achieving direction. It is the tool that provides you the compass to help find and experience a life well lived. It is about becoming an exceptional person who leads others to becoming extraordinary along with you. Remember, the 4 Most Important Questions of direction are vital to the journey.

> *Commit them to heart and they will not fail you.*

CHAPTER ONE

Will Changing Your Attitude Change Your Life?

How changing your flawed thinking will get you everything you want.

In my experience, I have learned that *direction is more important than a good attitude.* Don't get me wrong, a good attitude is important. I don't want to say you shouldn't manage your attitudes. We all know how hard it is to work around someone with a bad attitude. However, if attitude was all you needed to adjust, how is it that a person with a bad attitude can still get things done?

A good attitude by itself is not enough to attract everything you want into your life. What I am saying is *tie your good attitudes to a precise, focused, clear direction.* Begin moving toward those things you desire. You then will experience the right activities bring about the right results. This directed energy will open up all kinds of possibilities for you to achieve those things that give you meaning and purpose.

I also have found that *enthusiasm without a clear direction is a delusion.* It takes common sense to choose the right direction. Choose the right direction or you will end up feeling lost and defeated. You cannot afford to present the *false impression* that everything is going to turn out okay. Thinking a good attitude alone will influence and change all that's wrong is a poor philosophy. Family, friends, and work associates may think you are really something because you seem so positive.

Excitement without a clear direction is like the fighter pilot who asks his navigator, "Where are we?" The navigator says, "I don't know Sir, but we are making good time." You can't afford to be moving six-hundred miles an hour and not know where you came from or where you want to go. The navigator must have an ongoing, tightly, focused awareness of the mission. He must constantly be asking all 4 Most Important Questions. First, *where am I going?* Second, *why is going there important?* Third, *who is going with you?* Fourth, *how am I going to get there?* Without a clear ongoing attentiveness to these 4 Most Important Questions, they cannot achieve the mission they've been assigned and get back to their base safely.

Just as it is for the pilot and navigator, it is equally important for you to have the right life map and know how to use it. While a good attitude is important, it won't attract the things into your life that you want unless you have a clearly defined direction to get them.

If you don't ask the 4 Most Important Questions, it doesn't matter at what speed you are moving. You are never going to find the path that will take you where you want to go. Things in the universe will never open their doors for you. Consequently, you will end up drifting along while not being able to attract what you want into your life. Okay, so you are not a pilot of a fighter jet, and you are not moving six-hundred miles per hour. Still, you have a limited time here on earth. I'm suggesting right now that you begin to pay attention to these 4 Most Important Questions for your life. Otherwise, those few failures allowed into your life every day will soon become a huge pile amounting to a big mess, robbing you of joy and personal fulfillment.

Why is direction more important than activity?

Success is the right activity in the right direction for the right reason.

As you begin down your path toward the success you want, remember *don't mistake activity for achievement.* They are not equal. For example, you can be busy making figure eights on the hockey rink. You even can be working up a sweat, but you will not be scoring any goals. The bottom line is you are not accomplishing what is important to the team at the time. Your teammates won't think you are of much uses either. Consequently, it is very important for you not to be stuck in the trap of measuring activity for achievement. They are just not the same. Success is the right activity in the right direction for the right reason. The right activity will bring into your life everything you want. Hoping the universe will open up its doors to you just because you want something is magical thinking. This kind of assumption won't work unless it is accompanied with the right activity pointing you in the right direction. Otherwise, you will end up frustrated, empty handed, and questioning why life is not working out for you!

Only you can determine what will create happiness for you.

Why is direction more important than purpose?

Also, remember that *direction is more important than purpose.* You can be very passionate about a significant cause. However, if you lack a clear direction to carryout that purpose, the passion will die a slow steady death. Again, the 4 Most Questions are the most critical factors to consider. Passion needs a disciplined direction to succeed or it cannot be achieved.

An important element to reading a map and beginning a journey is to know where you are starting and where you want to go. It is the same for you right now in choosing a new direction for your life. Unless you can answer these 4 Most Important Questions I've set before you, then you won't find the path that leads you to a life of joy and purpose.

So, the first step is to admit where you are at right now. If you are broke, you need to admit it. If relationships around you are shattered, you need to admit it. If you feel like you are in a dead end career, you need to admit it. If your health is pounding on you because you have neglected it, you need to admit it.

You can't begin to change what you don't acknowledge. This is very hard for many people. It is easier to pretend you know where you are. You pretend you know where you are going. You pretend rather than admitting you don't really have a clue. You don't want to face how lost you are. You continue to pretend that the rules by which you run your life are getting you what you want. You pretend that no one is keeping score and others' opinions don't matter. You pretend the maps you have been following clearly lead you where you want to go. You pretend everything is okay and your life is good. You pretend the people following you are following you because you know which path to take. You pretend, you pretend, you pretend . . .

This book is about your facing the truth of where you are in relationship and getting where you want to be. It is all about creating a turning point. It is making choices to change your life around to achieve an extraordinary one. It is about taking the courage to face the truth about your life. It is confessing to yourself you have been pretending everything is all right when it not! It is about owning the problem differently. It is about making choices to change. It is choosing to live to your highest and best ability. It comes about first by you being honest with yourself.

Only you can determine what will create happiness for you. Only you can align the internal compass in your life to the principles and *True North* laws of relationships and self-management. Only when you realize that you alone must face and struggle with these 4 Most Important Questions are you ready to achieve all the things that are truly priceless to you. No one else can choose your direction for you, but others can help. *This is the intention of this book.*

Why is it so important to surround yourself with really quality people?

This book is about determining who travels with you on the path you choose. It is about discovering how you will get there. The pages of this book are about applying essential fundamental strategies to achieving enjoyment and a successful, rewarding life. Why is this important you may ask? It is important because you can then achieve an exceptional life for yourself.

Now get ready, because you are going to learn how to find the things valuable and important to a life filled with meaning and purpose. First, you must set the internal compass within yourself. Unless this compass follows the *True North Principles* of relationships and self-management governing all of life and living, you will never have more than an ordinary life. You never will experience being extraordinary, and you never will move into the realm of a fantastic life of personal delight and intention.

The Principle Of *10 times* The law of repetition	*Why is it so important to teach this stuff to someone else?*

We will pause at the end of each lesson for a brief reflection on the material you just read to ask what it is that you have learned. I believe in the *Principle of 10 times*—the law of repetition. Apply this principle by taking something you learned in this lesson. Teach it to 10 people. Each person you teach will get the benefit of it once. Teach it to 10 people, and it will become anchored in your value system. You then will be able to remember it. Once you adapt it as one of your building blocks, it will help you live a successful life of lasting importance. Are you ready? Here we go on a journey of excitement and life change!

Remember, it is easy to pass up the questions at the end of each chapter. No one is keeping score on you. However, I suggest you take time to go through these questions one by one. Give them some deep thought. Why is this so important? It is important because you won't achieve a turning point for your life unless you do. In fact, I suggest you ask someone important to you to give you feedback. Ask them how they think you are doing. What are their answers as they have observed your behavior and listened to your thinking?

Choose today to set a new course for your life. It is your life. I suggest you make the decision right now to set the internal compass of your life to a new direction. Do it so that you attract into your life everything that is of great importance to you. Take out a piece of paper and write down today's date. Then write these words: "Today I choose to set a new course for my life." Writing it down will make you own it differently. Why is that true? It is true because it is easy to pass it by and not put an importance to really committing to being different and changing. Writing it down will help you admit it is vital to lasting change. It will help you be one of those individuals who really achieve lasting change in their life.

Are you ready to set the course to be, to do, and have all the significant things of lasting importance you want for your life? Well, here we go!

1. Take out a new sheet of paper. Write down today's date, ___/ ___/____.

2. Write out the phrase, "Today I choose for myself to set a new course for my life." Sign your name to the page. Why is that so important? It is important because you are making a contract with yourself. Everybody knows a contract isn't good until you sign it. So, sign your name. Make a contract today with yourself to begin a new journey to achieve the most fantastic life only you could imagine.

3. On the same piece of paper, write down your age. If this assignment scares you, put it in some kind of code in case it should fall into the hands of someone who might use it against you. ____. ☺

4. Take that number and subtract it from 90, and the difference is an estimate of how many years you have left to live. Write that number down, ____. It is important. It is not a guarantee you will live that long, but it is very important for making a life plan. This represents the estimated number of years you have left.

5. Now project yourself forward and attend your own funeral. Show up in the back of the room and take a seat. What is it

you want them to say about you? As you listen to your family and friends, what do they say you have accomplished? Listen to what they say about how you invested in your family and community. What do they say about the career you had while living your life? What do they say about how you got involved in your greater community? What mistakes do they say you made? I mean huge mistakes. What successes do they credit to you? How were you at giving and keeping your word? How do they think you did?

6. Now go to your attorney's office with your heirs that survived you. What does your attorney say about your estate? What plans have you placed into motion to protect those assets you acquired throughout your life and for those who will receive them? Why are these things important? On a scale of 1 to 10 with 10 being the highest, ask yourself, "How am I doing?"

7. Take your right hand. Put the thumb on your heart. Spread the fingers wide apart from each other. Now the thumb represents the person closes to your heart. Who is that person? Write their name down. Why are they so important? The index finger represents the next person of importance to you. Write their name down too. And so on down the hand. Tell the story about why these people are important to you. What are you presently doing for these people to help them feel they are valuable and important to you? If this were a court of law, would there be enough evidence from your behavior toward these people to prove what you claim you are doing to make them feel significant?

8. Now place your left hand on your heart. This time the thumb represents your career. Is it easy for you to get up each morning and on your way without dread? Does it touch your heart's passion and desire? Does it tap your talents and leave you energized or frazzled? Let the index finger represent

your savings and investments. (I think there is something wrong when an adult works for 40 years and does not have enough savings and investments on which to live comfortably in retirement.)

Let the middle finger represent your health. Do you have a wellness plan that will carry you into your retirement and beyond? How is your health? Is it at risk because you have been neglecting it for years? Let the ring finger represent friendships beyond your family. Do you have friendships that enrich your life and help you stretch and continue to grow? Do you have a person outside of the family who lets you be yourself even though they know your weaknesses and flaws? Let the pinky finger represent your continued intellectual enrichment and ethics. What would your friends say about how trustworthy you are? Remember, trustworthy is being worthy of trust. How are you at making and keeping your word?

How are you doing on your way to achieving the things you want for yourself? After sitting through your own funeral and the attorney's office, you may ask yourself, why does it matter what others think of me? It matters because it is a report of how you have lived your life. It is a tool to measure how effective you have been in the pursuit of what you count as those things, which are truly significant.

9. Okay, let's go back to the present. With the years you have left, what are you going to do with them that will make you an outstanding individual people will value?

10. Here is a warning! Be careful who you become in the pursuit of what you think you want. Why should we be concerned? Sometimes we go after things at the cost of significant relationships, our reputation, or our health. It would be just

as sad to die labeled successful, but have no one at our funeral or to die early because we put a higher priority on work than the daily routines of eating well and exercising.

11. Here is a tough assignment. What have you been pretending is okay? Is it your career? How is your marriage? How is your health? How are the relationships with your children? Are you pretending you are important while feeling insignificant? Superiority is the first red flag of inferiority. Are you pretending you are happy when you aren't? You can change all that and find an amazing life. On the other hand, you can continue to use lots of energy pretending everything is okay. You can go on presenting a false self to the world so people won't find out about the real you, but they always will. On the other hand, you can make a choice right now to change and become something different. The choice is yours.

12. Okay, get ready to ask yourself the 4 Most Important Questions.

13. The first and most important question is, where am I going? What do you want to attract into your life? If there were no restrictions, what would you want?

14. The second question is, why is going there so important to me? The why you want something is very important. If the why is big enough, it will pull you along.

15. The third question is, who is going on the journey with me? Nobody gets anything done without building a great team. What talents and gifts do you want these people to bring with them to help you accomplish everything you want?

16. The fourth question is, how are you going to get there? Clearly identify where it is you want to go. Then you must identify why it is important to go there. Once you choose the team to help get you get there, it opens the door to attracting those things into your life. But wait! This is not enough! It takes your asking, how am I going to get there? Once you begin moving toward those wants, they open endless ideas on how to get them. Then begin acting upon those ideas and it helps you attract them into your life. It is that simple.

17. You may not just yet be able to answer the 4 Most Important Questions You Can Ask Yourself. This is okay. I challenge you to continue to read on, so that you can find the answers and put into practice the strategies to create a fantastic life for yourself. I also suggest you set a time in your calendar to come back to this chapter, read it again, and give yourself more time to answer the questions outlined in this chapter.

Wait! We aren't yet finished. Keep reading! There are several important principles ahead of you in this book. You also will need to incorporate them into your thinking in order to achieve lasting change. So let's move on and find out what they are.

CHAPTER TWO

Why is the best day of your life—the day you get whatever you wish for—also the worst day?

Who Wrote the Word **LOSER** on Your Forehead?

Okay, I'm assuming you've read this far because you want something different for your life. I presume you are looking for the right switch to click so that it all makes sense to you. Well, I believe the place to begin to attract everything you want into your life starts with your own private world. If your private world is in disorder, your public world will reflect that same turmoil. If you have an honesty problem with others, you are only reflecting an honesty problem from within yourself. If you are selfish and unfair with others, you are only reflecting the character flaw of your need to be right. This flawed thinking usually ends up costing you everything priceless and dear to you, especially your integrity. It will keep you from experiencing a life of joy and personal fulfillment.

...the way to true freedom comes through organizing your private world first.

The lack of outward self-discipline in your life is only a reflection of the inward expressions of the lack of self-discipline. It is impossible to live a private life filled with deceit and deception, while portraying a public life of honesty and integrity. Eventually your flawed thinking and character will spill into your public world. It will cause huge hurt to yourself and others you value. I have found the failure to stay connected to others in a healthy way is only a reflection of the feelings of failures in your own private world. Living like this will make you spend a lot of time pretending to look good. Pretending takes energies that could help you bring order into your own private world.

These truths are foundational to having an influence in your outer world. You cannot reverse this and achieve the balance necessary to be, to do or to have an amazing life. You will end up giving away your personal power and influence with others. You fail in self-expression and experience the loss of freedom to live a fantastic life. Thus, the way to true freedom comes through organizing your private world first. This is the true path toward a life that is well lived.

The oldest and greatest fallacy in human thinking traps you by the belief *"that who I am in my public world won't be affected by who I am in my private world."* You lead yourself to believe that they are two separate things. You deceive yourself with this contrived thinking. This fallacy will get you nowhere fast. You might just as well stamp on your forehead in big, black capital letters the word **LOSER**.

The story of *The Goose and the Golden Egg*

Do you really believe you can attract into your life all the things you desire? Do you believe it is possible to change and become the kind of individual others want to follow? For you to become the best individual you can become, you need a new formula to achieve it. If you truly believe this, you must first start making changes on the inside in order to attract the changes you want on the outside. You cannot reverse this principle and achieve success. This book is about an inside-outside formula that leads you along the path toward learning the strategies of an incredible life. To understand this, we begin with the fable of "The Goose and the Golden Egg."

This fable is a story about a farmer and his goose. The story starts with the farmer going down to the goose's nest one morning to gather an egg for his morning breakfast. Then one particular morning, he reaches into the nest and finds a rather large, heavy golden egg. Thinking it has no value, he throws it into the bushes as he walks back to the house, mumbling to himself that he won't have his usual breakfast to eat.

Over time, he begins to think about the golden egg. The more he thinks about the egg, the more he believes that he should have it evaluated. He retrieves the egg from the bushes and takes it into town to be examined. In town, he finds that the egg is pure, solid gold. He cashes in on the value of the golden egg for money and comes home quite happy. So each morning, he goes down to the goose's nest and finds one egg made of solid gold just like the first one he found. Then each day he takes the golden egg to town and exchanges it for money. Over time, he becomes very rich.

Then one day, he decides it is too much work for him to go down to the goose's nest each morning to get the daily golden egg. He comes up with the idea that he can kill the goose, cut off its head, and reach inside of its belly to get all the golden eggs out at once. He draws the conclusion that this is a great idea to save time. He feels that he now has earned the right to take a rest. After all, he has become rich. He now feels that he is above the task of gathering one measly golden egg each day. In his decision to kill the goose, the farmer failed to realize he has a flaw in his long-term thinking. His short-sited decision means he no longer will have the goose to supply him with more golden eggs. He doesn't care, because he has grown tired of the process of dealing with the whole thing.

See, the farmer somewhere along the way, forgot what really was most important to him. Somewhere he got lazy. Somewhere he lost sight of the worth of the goose giving him the golden egg each morning that provided him his wealth. Somewhere in his pursuit of getting all the things he felt mattered, he forgot how important the goose was. He forgets the goose was the vehicle for him to get all the golden eggs he wanted.

Self-examination is the true path to greatness.

The truth is this, "If you don't take care of your goose, you don't get any golden eggs." So, we want to ask ourselves these questions:

1. What represents the goose in your life that will give you all the things that matter? Take time to make a quick outline of those things. They are the tools like your education, your health, your job, your customers or co-workers. They are your products or services that meet many people's needs. These tools are the vehicle that represents the goose that lays the golden eggs.

2. What represents the golden eggs in your life that will bring you personal fulfillment and joy? The farmer created wealth from the goose that gave him the golden eggs. If you became wealthy, what would you do with it? If you had the money, where would you travel? If money were not an object, what would you buy? What charity would you get involved in to help others less fortunate? Now that you have lots of free time, what are you going to do with it?

3. *"The best day of your life may be the day you get whatever you wish for; it could also be the worst day."* Why? Sometimes when you get what you want, you pay too high a price in fractured and estranged relationships or ruined health. Sometimes there is moral failure attached to it. The scandal ruins our reputation and damages our influence with those who matter the most.

4. "What mistakes are you making in taking care of your goose? Here is a wise precaution regarding the goose in your life: A few errors in judgment practiced every day pile up and soon you have a big messy pile in front of you. You kill the goose."

5. "Are you pursuing the golden eggs at the expense of the goose? Here is how to correct the problem. A few disciplines practiced daily also pile on top of one another and offset the messy pile. With those daily disciplines in place, you are on your way toward achieving everything you value and desire as truly important. You start getting the golden eggs you want."

6. Do you get it? The better you take care of the goose, the more golden eggs you can manage.

7. Ellie, a friend of mine, said, "It is simple 5th grade math." In basic terms, it adds up to being *no healthy goose, no golden eggs.*

8. Let's begin with the deeper, life changing questions. Have you been pretending everything is okay in your life? Have been deceiving yourself and others that everything is okay when it is not?

9. Have you bought into the myth: "*What I do in my private life doesn't affect my public world?*"

10. Have you looked in the mirror lately? Do you feel like a LOSER? Then it is time to make a decision to be different. Admitting to yourself your disappointment and failure is the first step toward getting the golden eggs you want. *What you acknowledge, you can change.*

11. What are the changes you need to make so you can be, have, and do the things that will lead you to living the life you want?

Okay, you have read this far for a reason. *Self-examination is the true path to greatness.* How, do we get the golden eggs we want? Let's continue reading and find out.

CHAPTER THREE

| Why is My Nest Always Empty of the Golden Eggs I Want? | Why isn't this attracting thing working for me? |

This question is almost as old as time. In fact, some of you will probably say, "I've heard all this stuff before." You will use it for an excuse to tune me out. You will make the error and decide to set down the book, and to stop reading it. Yet others will continue on to find deep life-changing truths. They will improve their relationships. They will finally achieve success in their career. Their home life will improve. They will step over into a life full of joy and purpose.

Some of you will move on to become a person of significant influence for generations to come. You may ask me, "Why is this? Why do people respond this way?" Well, it is a mystery. No one really knows why some people respond negatively, and others launch out into new dimensions of self-insight. They find truths that expand their growth toward becoming something surprisingly astonishing.

I like to compare this mystery to a combination lock on a safe. There are about twelve numbers to the combination lock to get the door open. Some people only need a few more turns of the tumbler and the door opens. Others think they have all the answers. They don't feel you can teach them anything new. They think I am just another person with the same old tune and message packaged differently. They are skeptical. They are the kind of people with their drinking glass half-empty rather than half full. I don't know why they are that way.

We can spend a lot of our time researching this phenomenon to try to understand, but it won't change them. We just have to place it in the arena of a mystery. So the first question you need to ask is in which group do you find yourself? Are you in the half-full group or the half-empty group? Choose wisely. It is your life.

I'll tell you what. I decide quickly which groups are the skeptics and get past these negative thinking, pessimistic people and move on to the ones who want to learn. The old ancient philosophy is true, *"when the student is ready the teacher will arrive."* You cannot teach a person who doesn't want to be taught. However, when a person is ready and willing to be taught, even a small child can teach you deeply significant things.

It is also just as true that you can't sell someone something when they aren't buying. You can be a gifted presenter of your product or service, as well as the best persuader. However, if they aren't buying, you are wasting your time and energy. So, it is important to determine quickly which crowd you are addressing. Why, you may ask? It is so you can get past those who will waste your time and on to those who are ready to buy.

I have talked to many people across my career as a speaker and executive coach. They have varied in age from children to teenagers, adults, and even retired people. It is just amazing to me who tunes you in and who tunes you out. You can spend your time getting mad at the ones who won't listen to your pitch or you can move past them to people who are open to your message, product, or service. It is your choice and *you get to choose your reaction.*

People have been trying since the beginning of recorded history to figure out how to get all the best opportunities for themselves.

In other words, what is success? How do you measure it? How can you achieve it fast?

> There is a truth here. The answers belong to those who look for them.

In addition, they have been writing it down ever since. Some of them even have learned how to get you to show up and pay a hefty price to hear what they have to say. Nothing is wrong with that happening. In fact, a good idea can be worth millions. I have come across a couple of people who gave me priceless pieces of information for which I would have paid huge amounts because it was so valuable. It was life changing to me. It created a turning point for me to become something more and greater than I would have been before they took the time to share with me. And I want you to know that I got what they said.

There is a truth here. The answers belong to those who look for them. If you are not looking, you won't recognize truth or the value of the person giving you the information in the first place.

Still, it remains a mystery why some people get it and others don't. Why is it that some people are ready for an opportunity whose time has arrived, while others let it pass them by without a second thought on what they might be missing?

Are you one of those people who let opportunity pass by you?

I think of my friend, Mark. He came to me in the early eighties. He wanted to know whether I had $5,000 to invest in a new venture with him. I want you to know that was when $5,000 was a considerable amount of my yearly income. He had teamed up with a new company that planned to sell purified water in small bottles for people to drink. "Mark," I said, "no one is going to buy distilled water in small bottles to drink when they can get all the clean water they want from the tap in their kitchen."

I laugh at myself when I think of what $5,000 of those early shares of stock would be worth today. Yet it is a perfect example of not being ready when an opportunity presents itself. It is an example of boxed-in thinking and the inability to read the buying migration trends for the future.

I remember Mark clearly saying, "Brad, in the future people will buy bottled water to drink." I remember looking at him skeptically. "No, really they will," he said. Well, Mark had eyes to read the future and I didn't. What a difference it would have made had I been a little more open to the teacher when he arrived. We can't beat ourselves up, because we all have these kinds of similar stories to tell.

On the other hand, we also all know someone who has been taken with what seemed too good of a deal to be true. They were snookered and it wasn't that good of a deal. So do your homework. Don't believe everything a seller tells you. Do your research and be diligent. Just don't stand still pretending the information is confusing when the independent research clearly points out that what is being said is true. Then you can make a choice about a wave of opportunity.

> …timing makes all the difference when it comes to profits.

You can choose to be out in front on the wave with all the energy behind you. You can choose to allow it to carry you along while everybody watches you zoom past. You can choose to wait for the calmer part wave to come along and hitch a ride in the safety of the back of the wave. You can choose to stand there wondering what in the world went by you. You get to make the choice on where and when you want to get involved. And your profits will be in direct proportion to your timing regarding the opportunity.

Let me tell you something, timing makes all the difference when it comes to profits.

What defines success for you?

So, what are your golden eggs? Is it a special kind of car and a big house in the best area of your city? Will it be a nice looking family and a great career? Are you driven to achieve that promotion at work? What about that corner office with the important title attached to the door? Will things be better because you get it? Are you looking to be famous and to achieve notoriety? How about accumulating a fortune others will envy?

Maybe you only need enough to feel safe and secure. Perhaps you prefer to be free to travel to exotic places and points of interest. Maybe all you want is to have enough money to spend time with the people you really love. Perhaps you want to have a shapely body that everyone envies. Only you can give the right answers to what you want to attract into your life. So, give some attention to the following questions and task. We can then move on to the *4 Major Life Alignments* necessary to achieving a life well lived in the following.

1. Have you attracted into your life all the golden eggs you feel you deserve?

2. If not, then take out a sheet of paper. Quickly jot down the things you want. Think about this: "*If time and money was no object, what would I really want for my life?*" Imagine you have all the money and time to achieve these things. Write it on your list. I can say that if it is important enough for you to write it down, it is important enough for you to get it. What you won't write down, you won't get! Writing it down will make

you own it differently. I remind you that you are doing this exercise because you want something different for your life. So, write down your wish list and think: "*What if I could have everything I put on my list?*" What would you include? The truth is that everything you write on your list you can have. Now, how important is the list?

3. Ask yourself this: "*Am I following the right crowd that will help me attract all the things I want in my life?*" You cannot master that for which you are not prepared. Sometimes we can't attract the things we want into our lives because of wrong associations. You hang out with a crowd that isn't going to help you get where you want to be. Now they maybe good people, but they won't help raise you to a higher level that will prepare you to attract the things into your life you really want. I don't suggest you cut them out of your life completely, but you might consider limiting your time with them. Time is the only thing you can't make more of for yourself. So, limiting some associations can help allow the space to attract the people into your life who can make it happen for you. These are the ones who have developed the life skills that can open doors by their connections. You need to include more time with this kind of person. Why is that important? Well, do you really want what is on your wish list or not? If it is not there as you are reading this material, then there is a reason for it. Examine the people you hang out with you. Ask yourself, "Are they the kind of individual who could handle millions if it came to them?" If not, you are hanging out with the wrong group.

4. Are you a skeptic or a student? Are you looking for your teacher or just chugging along waiting for something to fall into your lap? Start today and build a plan! Build a wellness plan. Build a wealth plan. Build a plan to expand your understanding. Build a spiritual, moral, and ethical plan that will draw others

to want to follow your example. These steps will lead people in the right path of living. Build a plan to take the steps that will inspire and challenge others to be extraordinary.

5. Name a couple of teachers who have come into your life. What did they teach you? Did you learn well the lesson they brought you? Have you passed it on to 10 other people? Do you remember the principle of 10 times from the first chapter? Take time to write those teachers a short note and thank them for taking the time to share with you. Let them know that you got it! Write the note even if you don't send it! The gratitude you express is an important factor in attracting more goodness into your life. I use a gratitude journal. I've committed to writing at least five things a day for which I am truly grateful. It is amazing how the pages accumulate. Reviewing each entry helps create within me a deepening sense of appreciation for the blessings in my life. Start today with your own gratitude journal. You will soon be truly amazed what other things it attracts into your life.

6. Identified the things you really desire to have, to be, and to do. Concentrate on identifying the golden eggs you want. Write them on cards, and put them around the mirror where you get ready in the morning. If they are important enough to write down, they are probably worth achieving. If they aren't, you won't write them down. And I bet you won't ever get them. Write this down: "*I want to be a millionaire.*" You may say that you don't need to be asked if you want to be a millionaire. Of course you do! So, write it down! Every person I know who is a millionaire, at some point, wrote it down.

Let me also give you a warning. Just realize that it is one skill to become a millionaire and another to hold on to that million. You have to learn and acquire both skills. Don't be so naive to believe that your ability and skills automatically enable you to be able to invest wisely and keep your millions. Look at pro athletes. How many athletes, once paid millions for the talent they brought to their sport, are now broke? How many lottery winners are in the same boat? The statistic shows that most go bankrupt within three to five years after winning millions. The percentage is huge.

7. Be honest with yourself. What side of the wave are you riding? Are you out in front or do you wait for calmer waters? Maybe you are one of those individuals who wonder what in the world just went by you.

8. What would a golden egg look like if it showed up? Let me tell you! We have been talking about the nest only. You must first have a goose before you get the golden egg you want. Come on, where is your thinking? Some people can't get to where they want to be, because they don't have the proper vehicle to get them there. They trudge along in life like a caged hamster, rapidly running its wheel, going nowhere fast.

A vehicle represents one idea whose time has come. It can take just one idea. The law of attraction states that ideas will come to you faster than you can manage them. All you have to do is open yourself to the possibilities the universe has to offer and move toward achieving it. Once you do this, you open up unlimited opportunities of potential of golden eggs. Remember, you need a healthy goose to get your golden eggs. The goose represents the vehicle to attract the golden eggs your want. So you need a plan to get and take care of that goose!

Let's move on to the next lesson. We will discuss how to begin the process of working on the inside to achieve balance in your outer world. Don't skip this chapter, because balance is necessary. The spiritual, moral, ethical balance is the foundation upon which you will stack your golden eggs when they arrive. If your foundation is weak, you won't be able to recognize or handle the goose when it shows up. Nope! The opportunities will pass right by you and you won't even realize it. Now, if you find yourself stuck here, keep reading because the path to filling the nest with all the golden eggs you want is just ahead in the next chapters.

CHAPTER FOUR

What are the things I can do to get ready to receive my golden eggs?	Could You Be the One Standing in the Way of Your Own Success?

The *First* of the **4 Major Life Alignments**
Being spiritual, moral, ethical, character, and integrity centered.

When I begin teaching this section at a seminar, I ask everyone in the room to humor me for a few seconds by closing their eyes. Then I ask them to point with their index finger where they think north is and hold their fingers in place. Once this is accomplished, I ask them to open their eyes. When they look around the room, they see people pointing in all different directions. It's an exercise that gets laughs, but it leads to an important point. I tell them:

You are the one trying to find change in your life.

This is why you have come to this room.

You are looking for answers of how to change yourself.

You are here to learn how to begin to attract into your life all the things you desire.

You want the good life, but there seems to be some confusion among us who knows which direction is the right path.

If north represents success and you disagree where north is, how are you supposed to trust who can point you in the direction to find your own success?

At that point, I take out a real compass and place it in my left hand. I turn to face the direction the compass needle tells me is north. Pointing with my hand I tell them, "this is north." Then I correct the base of the compass with the letter N to match the direction of the needle the compass shows as pointing north. As I point north, I say, "The base and the needle are now both aligned to north. This way is north."

They, of course, agree. I then turn the base of the compass so that the needle and the N are no longer aligned. I tell them that the N on the base of the compass says this is now north. Point with my hand I say, "this way is now north, right?"

> The truth is aligning you life to the internal compass of character and integrity gives your behavior and thinking direction.

Everyone agrees that it is not north, nevertheless, I restate that the "N" on the bases says, this is now north, so it has to be north. As I expect, my audience tells me that "N" on the compass base has nothing to do with the needle, which still points north. Again, they are correct, North is a fixed

"N" on the compass base has nothing to do with true north's direction. It does not determine north. This point that does not change. The illustration represents a truth that also should guide your life.

The truth is, aligning your life to the internal compass of character and integrity gives your behavior and thinking direction. Just as the compass needle always points toward north, so should the principle of character and integrity define and guide your life. The foundation of it is character, integrity, and morals expressed as your ethics. You can use it as a fixed point for your behavior and thinking to provide you a quality for a life full of joy and purpose. I call this spiritual aligning, *The True North Principle.*

Perhaps you have had the same trouble I have had when my behavior doesn't align with what I value as important. When this happens, I find myself in a predicament. I find myself explaining my way out of it!

Not aligning your life to this *True North Principle* and the laws that govern all of life and relationships creates huge failures for you. On top of this, you will create pain for those who love and value you. Being out of alignment with the *True North Principle* will mess you up and keep the law of attractions from working for you. In the end, you won't get those things you count as truly priceless.

In the areas of what really matters, the neglect of your spirituality makes you lose sight of what has lasting importance. You end up surrendering things that you should not lose. When you neglect your spirituality, you lose an important aspect of a balanced life and achieving a life well lived.

So how do I set the internal compass of my life?

You may tell yourself that spirituality isn't that important—at least not right now. It might be important sometime in the future, like when you finally face your own death. The fact is, you don't see yourself as dying, though you might acknowledge it in your mind. So you put off examining your spiritual self, because death doesn't seem to be pounding on you today. In doing so, you dismiss the importance of what spirituality really is.

Some have bought into the belief that character and morality are old ways of thinking, not relevant for today's world. With this way of thinking governing your behavior, you will begin to pretend your life is doing just fine, when it isn't. You dismiss or neglect to follow the internal principles of character and the laws of relationships that govern everything you do. Soon, your self-esteem, marriage, children, career, and community life begin to suffer. You exceed the proper bounds of the *True North Principle* of character, integrity, and morality as important life-centering directives.

> You spirituality is the first of the 4 Major Life Alignments that make up the foundational block of your life on which everything else is built.

With this in mind, the *First of the 4 Major Life Alignments* is your spiritual, ethical, moral self. Knowing this means, you must give attention to the first life alignment before you do the second, third, and so forth. It is the same in construction. We must set the foundations of a house before you assemble the floors, walls and roof. Your spirituality is the first of the *4 Major Life Alignments* that make up the foundational block your on which everything else is built. This is like a square where each angle must be in constant harmony with the others for you to secure and hold the golden eggs you want. I believe that all other things will die and vanish, but that which is spiritual is eternal. It lives on beyond the scope of this reality you and I now experience as human beings. You cannot surrender or compromise this important dimension. It has essential lasting purpose that gives us true balance.

Ignoring or dismissing the importance of spirituality eventually affects your daily interactions with others. It eventually will spill out and reveal the internal flawed character in your spiritual, moral, and ethical nature.

> For you to make life work, you must come to grip with the question of where you are going.

You may be able to hide it for a while, but eventually its ugly head will show up for what it really is. And the undisciplined spiritual, ethical, moral nature is a very ugly thing indeed. It is my belief that no matter what your religious or spiritual views may be, you will want to take the time to evaluate your values, traits, and motives.

You may see yourself as being neutral or not believing in God. Spirituality is just not something you feel has any benefit for you. I would say this is false thinking. It has been the downfall of generations of leaders since the beginning of recorded history. If you too hold it as not being that important, then it is also a flaw in your thinking. The flaw will eventually create a huge gap in your behavior. It will lead you to significant hardships. The error in your thinking will not only block the law of attraction from working for you, but also hurt those who love and value you as someone significant.

As a spiritual and moral being, you have stamped within you the need to find meaning and purpose in your life. You naturally seek reasons for being here. You want to invest your time and talents in the world and make a difference. For you to make life work, you must come to grip with the question of *where you are going*. You must come to a clear conclusion to *why going there is important*. You have to choose a strong team of individuals *who will help you get there*. Above all else, you need to know *how you are going to get there*. Then this will give you lasting meaning.

> I believe living intentionally gives direction and purpose to your life.

Here is a truth, you are born and you will die. You are probably saying to yourself, "Well that's nothing new." Precisely! The important thing is that you have an amazing life to live in between those two events. It's how you live your life that makes the difference. And if you haven't gotten this yet, *that's why I've written this book.* It is up to you to find and make meaning of the time between your birth and death. It is hard to believe, but most people find this to be a difficult task! Few people realize that they can structure their lives, and find purpose, passion, and a deep well of meaning. It is within the scope of this truth that you give attention to a life plan for yourself.

Why is it so important to live an intentional life?

I believe living intentionally gives direction and purpose to your life. Building an intentional life plan will help you find meaning as you design your new life. Don't merely leave it up to chance. No! Live a purpose driven life! Decide today, this very moment, to create a turning point for yourself that will move your life into the arena of the extraordinary. How? You accomplish this by being aware that life is a sacred gift. It is short and to be esteemed as something precious.

Let's suppose you were given a week to live. What are you going to do with those precious hours you have left? Most of you don't see your life ending anytime soon. Consequently, you live without giving much attention to the daily details of your own existence.

Viewing your life as a sacred gift defines your purpose and passion. You begin to live intentionally by learning the significance of forgiveness and loving. Otherwise, you are stuck in anger while looking for revenge. You need to soak up and learn from each relationship and experience that touches you.

You live now! You live as though tomorrow holds no guarantees, obligations, or concerns. You do not pull yesterday's hurts and failures into today. You don't beat yourself up over past failures or blame others for the hurts they have caused you. You do not rob today by crowding it with tomorrow's worry, but you take care of each day's concerns today. Do these things and you will discover and live a fantastic life.

Putting your inner world in order and striving for a *purpose-driven life* is a journey and not a destination point. You begin the process by studying the sacred as the first step in balancing your life. However, you know this is a life-long process of perfecting and achieving, while allowing mistakes and creativity. This process makes room for reflection and introspection. It allows for committing to investigating what creates awe in you. Built upon the foundations of harmony found in all cultures, it is relationally the sum of all its parts like a well-balanced eco system.

You exercise healthy boundaries in pursuit of accomplishment. You find the balance between achievement and burnout. You are not obsessed with holding the only truth while making others wrong. You are not exclusive of others because their cultures are different, but look for ways to be inclusive. You know the importance of valuing the differences of others. You find a way to keep justice and mercy in balance. You are not interested in manipulating or controlling others to achieve your own end. You express genuine, sincere, and passionate appreciation for all. Perhaps, most of all, placing order in your inner world is a commitment to investigating what creates awe within others.

I am not here to push what I believe as the way to achieve a richer, fuller life. However, as I stated before, I believe you need to examine how you have bought into the myth of being one "self" in your private, personal world, and another "self" in your public world. The result is a double life. You have to stop pretending everything is okay when it isn't. Pretending makes you not follow the principles of life and relationship. It makes you fail to follow God's spiritual, moral, and ethical plan as the path to purpose. Believing that what you do in private has nothing to do with who you are in public is just wrong thinking. It will result in a huge disaster and keep you from getting and holding the golden eggs you want to attract.

Why is it so important to be both inwardly and outwardly a person of character?

Let me tell you a story about a former business partner of mine. This story illustrates how our private and public lives intertwine. I met ("Don") when he was in the middle of a divorce from his second wife. I found out later the divorce was the result of his having an affair with a woman he had met in his church choir. That was a story in itself. It turned out that Don had a serious history of womanizing. If you are wondering what this has to do with a business relationship, stay with me.

> In being spiritual, you need ethics.

In time, he began sharing stories at work about his dating life. He told a female business manager and me about concurrently seeing, and having a sexual relationship with, three different women. Because we were in business together, I confronted Don about his behavior. He responded by telling me that what he did privately had nothing to do with how he performed his work. When I said to him that was a lie he was telling himself, he began swearing at me. I told him that "trustworthiness means being worthy of trust, and he was pretending to be one thing while in reality being an entirely different person." I told him "effective relationships begin with trust." Since Don could not acknowledge his dishonesty, I decided it was time to end the business relationship.

In being spiritual, you need ethics. Ethics have everybody's best interest in mind. They are the core of human dignity. Morals are how we practice what is in everybody's best interest. Ethics and morals are foundational to a lasting community. So what is moral? It is kindness and self-respect for yourself and others. It is what makes up the whole of our core values and gives self-respect. Respect is the centerpiece of making things work. Our core values flow into ethical expressions through respect for self and respect for others. Without respect, our society gradually will deteriorate. It might not be noticeable today, but like a corrosive acid, unchecked, it will end up destroying everything truly important.

Since *The first of the 4 Major Life Alignments* is *The spiritual, ethical, moral, and character area,* contemplate the following:

1. Let's review an earlier test: On a scale of 1 to 10 with 10 being the highest, how are you doing with those relationships represented by your right hand? Remember, I asked you to take your right hand and place the thumb on your heart. Then I had you to spread your fingers wide apart and identify whom your thumb represents. The thumb being the person closes to your heart. I asked you to tell why they were the closest to your heart. I also asked whether there was enough evidence in your behavior to convict you in a court of law on your claim. Could we really find enough evidence on you to prove you really treasure and adore the person you identified? Well, is there? Talk is cheap. How about asking them to give you a measurement of how they think you are doing in this area? Let them give you a number. Now, if that person says "3", don't argue. Instead, ask what it would take to move it from the 3 to 10. Listen to their response and take notes. Really, the number doesn't matter. What matters is how the person closest to you interprets what you do to make them feel valuable and important.

2. Teach someone *The True North Principle* of the laws that govern all of life and relationships.

3. How does giving attention to your spirituality set the internal harmony within you to achieve a life filled with meaning and purpose?

4.   How do you create a turning point for yourself and set your internal compass to *The True North Principles*?

5.   Why is your spiritual and ethical behavior so important to you making meaning out of where you are going? Why is it so important to answer the question of why you want to go there? How about its importance to who goes with you? Finally, why is it essential to how you are going to get there?

6.   Why should you concentrate on what is going on inside of you as the first step of achieving harmony and a life well lived?

7.   Why is respect for self and others the centerpiece of human dignity?

8.   What happens if you don't pay attention to your spirituality on the path to finding and living a life of meaning and purpose?

9.   What happens if you discount spirituality as not that important?

Okay, ready? Let's move on to the next chapter. There you can take a closer look at deeper questions you can ask yourself to help you *know* you are on the path to achieving spiritual balance for yourself.

CHAPTER FIVE

| Does it really affect my getting everything I want? | How Can I Get Together a Plan to Live Relationally? |

10 Principles to Aligning the Spiritual Compass of Your Life

Let's start out this section by posing a hypothetical question. If you were to jump off a 10-story building, what would happen to you? What would be the natural physical consequence of you making this decision? The answer should be obvious. We could call this a huge, dumb mistake, but the answer should be obvious. You would either permanently trash your health or physically destroy your life.

We have experience with gravity. We know that jumping off things over four or five feet can hurt us. We know and understand the principle of gravity. It is going to pull us down, and it doesn't matter whether I weigh 50 pounds or 250 pounds. If I jump off a 10-story building, I am going to hit the ground and be seriously hurt or killed. It doesn't matter whether or not I am educated. It doesn't matter whether I am wealthy or financially broke. I am going to hit the ground and get hurt or die. It doesn't matter whether I lived 500 years ago or 500 years in the future. If I jump off a 10-story building, the result will be the same.

Time does not change the principle, and the principle treats everybody the same.

There are all kinds of principles, and they govern all areas of our living. You can choose to operate within these principles or you can choose to violate them. The choice is yours, but the consequence remains the same. The decision will result in your being crushed or destroyed whenever you violate one of them. Why, you may ask? It is because they operate without respect to whom you are. A principle, like gravity, doesn't measure you and then decide to suspend its consequences just because you are someone nice or important. Nope! Principles are unbending. They are always in motion. You need to use them wisely, letting them guide you so that you can have this fantastic life we've been talking about.

I am no expert here, but let me give you 10 guiding relationship principles that have been given to me, which I believe are reasonable and applicable to all cultures. I have found them to be insightful for building and sustaining meaningful, lasting relationships. I have found wisdom and good common sense in the practice of following each of them. In addition, I have come to realize that they are a reflection of one's private spiritual world.

I call them a reasonable response to a life of character and integrity.

The principles of character and integrity are timeless. They are built on the foundation of trustworthiness. Being trustworthy is foundational to all cultures and is the mortar that holds a healthy, lasting society together. It is based upon your ability to give and

> The principles of character and integrity are timeless.

keep your word. People tend to count on the commitments you give to them. When you give and keep your word, you build huge reserves of trust. Trust is the foundation of relational living and a reflection of your spiritual health. The keeping of one's word really begins with one's self and expands into other relationships.

If you don't find these 10 principles helpful, I encourage you to continue searching until you find your own. Nevertheless, please let your paths follow these three steps: Learn, Apply, and Instruct. Don't just take my word. Research for yourself and draw your own conclusions. Once you have found solid lasting truth, apply it to your life. As you apply it to your own life, you should discover that it creates a door for you to walk through to begin the journey toward living the extraordinary life. As you apply this truth to your life, it will help you find lasting importance. In your searching, you should find that time doesn't change the principle. Finally, begin to instruct others on what you have found. Don't just keep it to yourself. No! Share it. True growth comes when you share. And that is what has lasting importance. If what you find isn't lasting truth, and the path you point people down doesn't help them achieve freedom to be extraordinary, then they won't show up.

It's important that we do not mistake sincerity with truth.

> Principles are time tested. They are universal to everyone and all cultures. Principles will not discriminate.

Anyone can be quite sincere and just as wrong. An example comes from the history of the church. It used to put people to death for holding certain beliefs that we now know as truth. One such belief the church held for centuries was that the earth was the center of the universe and everything seemed to revolve around us. It was easy to believe this way, because you could go out on any evening and see the sun set in the west. You could then see the moon and the stars slowly move across the sky. For years, the church held these observations to be truth, and it certainly was sincere about this truth. Though we now can laugh about how wrong those early dogmas were, but their truths then could mean life or death. For when someone came up with the idea that the world was round and spinning in a circle while orbiting the sun, he was told to renounce this new dogma or be put to death. The church was sincere in its belief, deduced from its observations, but it was wrong. Therefore, sincerity is not a test of truth. Do make sure the principles you hold as truth are time-tested, and not just something you hold and value sincerely.

Also, experience is not truth.

A magician can make you believe that something appeared or disappeared out of thin air. Your experience tells you that it happened. You witnessed it. So it must be truth. Don't be so naïve. While experience is helpful, it is not always governed by principles. Principles are time tested. They are universal to everyone and all cultures. Principles will not discriminate. They do not recognize the color of one's skin while discounting someone else, because of their culture or creed. Be certain you test your experience to make sure it holds up the principle as being time tested.

1. Why is a true principle timeless?

2. Are you allowed to violate timeless principles?

3. What is the natural consequence of violating a timeless principle?

4. Why is it important first to give attention to ordering your private spiritual life?

5. Why are the principles of character and integrity timeless?

6. Why is sincerity not a test of truth?

7. Why is experience not a test of truth?

8. Why must we keep our word in order to find a life of lasting importance?

9. Why must a principle be timeless to have lasting importance?

10. Why is it false thinking to hold to the position that "it doesn't matter what one believes as long as one believes and practices something?"

11. How do you set the spiritual compass of life so that you can find a life of true meaning and purpose?

So here is what I have found and hold to be the important, relational spiritual truth for aligning the spiritual compass of your life.

FIRST: *Be careful what you pursue as valuable and important.*	Principle # 1

You do this by making sure that it has lasting importance. Why you may ask? It is because, in the pursuit of what you feel you want, sometimes it costs you too much to achieve it. Why? Often getting or keeping what you want causes you to become someone whose behavior is ugly or shameful. Do you want to be remembered for ugly behavior toward others? Do you want to be a person who lives out a drama created from your indiscretions or your need to be right? Nope! It will leave you with feelings of humiliation and disgrace for yourself and those you value and love. You have a responsibility toward the greater good for all of humanity.

Remember, responsibility is the ability to respond well. So be careful what you pursue, because of who you become when achieving it. You might think it is valuable and important, only to find out in the end that the cost outweighed the value. The result is a huge messy pile. The high price robbed you of your health, assets, or valuable relationships. Sometimes pursuits without principles force people to have to live with a tragic story they created. Life is short. It would be sad to lean your ladder against a wall of success only to find out that it was the wrong wall. Equally sad is to spend your precious time and life energies trying to climb a ladder to nowhere. So when the final tally is counted, make sure what you pursue is priceless.

Jesus, The Master Teacher, told a story of two brothers and their father. The younger of the two brothers decided he didn't want to wait for his father to die to receive his inheritance. He asked his father to divide what he would inherit and he took off. Soon the son spent all his inheritance living a reckless, wild life. In fact, he slipped into deep poverty, even to the point of starvation. Overtime and after some deep reflection, the son made a decision to go back home. He concluded that it would be better to be a humble servant in his father's household than to waste away in extreme poverty.

When the son was near the front gate of the lane leading to the house, the father saw him coming. He came running down the lane and embraced his youngest son, who had found his way back home. The father then scheduled a party to celebrate his son's return.

Meanwhile, the older son had never asked for his inheritance. He had faithfully worked in the father's fields without the least disruption to the routines of the daily activities of the farm. When the older son learned dad was throwing a party for his younger, rebellious brother, he was very angry with his father.

The father went out to the field to discuss the situation with the older son and personally to invite him to join them at the party to celebrate the younger son's return. Because of all the poor decisions and wild living he knew the younger brother had done, the older brother could not allow himself to join the party.

> Ordering your private world begins with doing the right activity for the right reasons.

I share this story with you because I believe that we all are trying to find our way back to enjoying God's genuine, sincere, passionate love for our lives, while teaching others to find the same joy. That is what has lasting importance. Either you enjoy the fruit of this privileged relationship or you have not yet claimed its privilege. That, along with instructing others in its truth, is what lasting importance is all about.

Make a promise to yourself today to start with that activity, Write it down. There is something about making a commitment when you discipline yourself to write down the promise. Don't over promise, because you won't be doing it several weeks from now.

Ordering your private world begins with doing the right activity for the right reason. You don't have to have all of your spiritual life together, but you do need a plan to get it together. So start with a promise to yourself that you can keep, and then keep it.

Write it down. It only has to be one or two areas on which you commit to work. Simply start by making a commitment to start today. Make a promise to yourself you know you can keep. How hard can that be? Writing down the commitment makes you own it differently. It is easy to retract your commitments when you don't write them down. So list the areas you want to improve in your spiritual journey.

1. Why is it so important to be careful that what you pursue has lasting importance?

2. What is the cost for pursuing something that doesn't have lasting importance?

3. What are you pursuing and what is it making of you in your pursuit of it?

4. What is it costing you in the health department?

5. What is it costing you in the asset department?

6. What is it costing you in your valuable relationships?

7. Is your life filled with much drama?

8. How do you measure your success?

9. Are you proud of the person you have become during the pursuit?

10. What are you pursuing that has lasting importance? Have you claimed your inheritance yet? Have you found your way back to God? Have you claimed the full benefits of being a son or daughter of God?

11. What is your responsibility to change your direction or the wall you have leaned your ladder against?

12. Why is spirituality the one thing that has lasting importance?

13. What spiritual activity, performed routinely would enrich your ability to enjoy the genuine, sincere, passionate love of God for yourself?

| **SECOND:** *Allow for awe in your life.* | Principle # 2 |

Make time to get in touch with the Creator of all things. We seem to lose site of the splendor that is ours. This joy can leave a lasting stamp of awe on us. Awe can be generated by the simplest of things, like observing and participating in nature. Experiencing awe does not have to be complex. It can be watching a sunrise or the birth of a newborn. It might be a meaningful relationship with someone. It is represented by a person who you feel safe to be open and emotionally honest.

I believe that as spiritual beings, we must routinely set aside time to honor God, and to worship Him. In the act of sacred worship, you take time to renew yourself by examining and ordering your private world. I have realized the importance of setting aside time to reflect on the directions you have taken and the paths you have followed. You need to go over the tapes in your minds and review the decisions you have or have not yet made. You need to see where you have come from and where you need to go. Why? So you can make important corrections in your paths If you don't take time to review and correct your path, you can drift off course and never arrive at your point of destination. You will end up pursing things you thought were valuable, but don't have lasting importance. You will end up settling for a good life instead of a great one.

Think of a rocket ship taking off for the moon. When the spaceship is launched, the first 3½ miles are the most difficult. The pull of the earth's gravity on the ship requires an extreme amount of thrust from the rocket's engines for the spaceship to break free of the earth's atmosphere. Once the ship is free, the pilot must correct its path, because the earth's gravity has changed its trajectory. It is called a mid-course correction. Without making a mid-course correction, the pilot would miss the moon. When you are aiming for the moon, you can't afford not to correct your path. So you must recalculate the moon's orbit and correct your spaceship's direction.

So it is with your life. You must periodically make a mid-course correction in your own life's path so that you arrive at the place for which you are aiming. How sad it would be to have the chance to live an unbelievable life, yet settle for a mediocre one.

In the pursuit of awe, keep in mind the necessity of taking care of and being responsible for the environment. You cannot lose sight of your greater responsibility to those who will follow. Caring for the environment lays the foundation for the future generations who will inherit and build upon what we have gained and learned. That means awe is not just enjoying splendor today, but making sure it is protected to be there for those that follow us. It is taking care of the goose so that the golden eggs keep coming.

Recently I received one of those touching forwarded emails we all seem to get from time to time. It related a story about a teacher who asked his students what they thought were the Seven Wonders of the World. There were some disagreements, but the following received the most votes: The Great Pyramids of Egypt, The Taj Mahal, The Golden Gate Bridge, The Panama Canal, The Empire

State Building, St. Peter's Basilica Chapel, and The Great Wall of China. As the teacher was completing the final tally of the votes, he noticed that one student had not finished.

"Are you having troubles with your list?" he asked the student.

"Yes, a little bit," the student replied. "I can't quite make up my mind, because there seems to be so many from which to choose."

The teacher said, "Well, tell us what you have on your list, and maybe we can help."

The student hesitated for a bit, then began to read: "I think the 'Seven Wonders of the World are: the ability to see, the ability to hear, the ability to have feelings, the ability to touch, the ability to laugh, the ability to taste, and the ability to love and be in love." When he finished reading his list, you could almost hear a pin drop.

Isn't it interesting that the things that you and I overlook as simple and ordinary and take for granted are truly wondrous! The ordinary can be extraordinary. They are gentle reminders that the most precious things in life cannot be built by human hands. Nonetheless, they fill us with true wonder and awe. So in all of your pursuing, allow for awe in your life. And remember to allow for the things that have true lasting wonder.

1. What creates awe in your life?

2. Why is it so important?

3. When was the last time you allowed this awe to enrich your life?

4. Do you have a routine time set aside to worship God?

5. How important is it to make corrections in the paths we follow?

6. Why is making a mid-course correction essential to living a fantastic life?

7. Why is being renewed so important to awe?

8. Why is awe so important to our private spiritual world?

9. Why is honoring God so important to awe?

10. Why is being too busy the thing that will crowd out honoring the Creator of all things?

11. What changes do you want to make in your life to allow for awe?

12. What difference might it make if you routinely allowed awe to be there?

13. Would your calendar reflect what you've just said? If not, then schedule it and take the time to be there?

THIRD: *Remember the importance of rest and reflection.*	Principle # 3

You accomplish this by giving yourself the time to stop and rest from being busy. You need to take a break in the routine of your working to just rest and recuperate. So often, I observe people who are just weary trying to do it all. They are endlessly pursuing the next project and not enjoying where they are currently. Life seems to be ahead, in the future, rather than in the here and now.

The endless pace is like the parents who have each of their children enrolled in a different sport. They find their weekends filled with rushing between games only to collapse at night in exhaustion from running around to all the kids' activities. Not to mention getting each child to and from practice once or twice through the week.

> So set aside time on a weekly basis for routine rest, and take some of that time to reflect.

Rest allows for a break in the routine of doing. It renews you so that you can reinvest your energies into the people and activities around you that truly have lasting importance. Rest and reflection allow you the time for serenity that will equip you to lead others to a great life. Otherwise, you will live a cluttered life. So set aside time on a weekly basis for routine rest, and take some of that time to reflect.

What rest and reflection looks like depends on the individual. For me, in addition to weekly rest and reflection, I also like to get away for about 4 days on a quarterly basis. I find that I need the time to go over where I have been and align myself to the direction where I want to go. We all have a tendency to drift off course and get distracted, well at least I do. My get-away works for me, but you need to find something that works for you and do it.

One February morning an exercise trainer where I routinely workout got into a conversation with me about the weather. It had snowed seven inches the night before in the Chicago area. She was complaining about being cold, and how she couldn't wait for spring to arrive so that she could get outdoors again.

Without dismissing her feelings, I told her that I had experienced the snowfall differently. I said that I had spent a couple of hours last evening just watching the big beautiful flakes of snow falling gently against the trees, covering the sidewalks, streets, lawns, and the houses in my neighborhood. I remarked that I found it just a wonder of creative beauty to observe. I said, "I think only God can create that kind of splendor."

As our conversation continued, I learned that she liked hiking. So after listening to her for a while, I suggested that she put together a plan for this time next year to take a hiking trip in a warm climate, such as Arizona or New Mexico. I also suggested that she plan now for the trip next year and to put it on her calendar or it wouldn't happen. I knew that if she didn't place enough importance on it to put it on her calendar, the year would quickly slip away, and so would many more to follow. I knew that she would one day look back and regret that she never included the most wonderful hiking breaks she could imagine.

Create a plan now to include important breaks in your busy schedule or they won't be there. If you don't make a plan, you will find that life's busyness will crowd out the valuable and important things for those things that don't have lasting importance.

1. What importance do you place on rest and reflection in your schedule? Does your calendar reflect that importance? Would those closest to you say you have this in balance? Would you be willing to ask their opinion on the subject?

2. Why do you think that breaks in the routines of being busy help put your spiritual life in order?

3. How do you take these breaks?

4. When was the last one you scheduled?

5. What valuable and important thing did you discover that brought you lasting importance?

6. When is the next one you have scheduled? Is it on your calendar yet?

7. Where are the places you go to get renewed? Why?

8. Do you find your life cluttered with being too busy pursuing things? Are you making excuses for why you can't find time to get away? Do you think your world would fall apart if you scheduled a time to get away?

9. When you are away is your mind still back at work?

10. What is your formula for scheduling rest and reflection for yourself?

11. What commitments do you need to make to yourself and to those valuable relationships for you "to be there?" Without a commitment to rest and reflection, you may be surprised by a health problem ahead of you, and it will pound on you to make you rest. Listen to your body before it demands your attention!

FOURTH: *Show genuine, sincere respect toward yourself and others.*	Principle # 4

You accomplish this by truly seeing every person as a unique individual instead of an extension of yourself. It is easy to show respect to those who agree with you, complement your way of life, your value systems, and that which you prize or hold as important. On the other hand, it is harder to show respect to those who are vastly different than you. Their habits, culture, and ideals seem to conflict with what you think and hold as valuable and important. Here is one that is even more difficult. It is especially hard to show respect toward someone who has hurt you deeply. Worst yet, what if they continue to hurt you again and again, and don't seem to care about what they are doing or have done.

If you have one of these hurtful people in your life, it is important to take time to enter into an act of forgiveness toward that person for the hurt they have inflicted into your life. I am not suggesting that you need to sit down on a weekly basis and have lunch together, be buddies, or even make contact. What I am saying is that you need to decide to deal with the hurt rather than drag it around with you every place you go.

Sometimes in your self-dialogue, you rewind those painful tapes over and over again, rehearsing the hurt, talking about the wound, playing the part of the victim, or living out the martyr's cycle in our head. You rob today of today's energy with wounds from the past. Sometimes the self-dialogue being played in your mind emerges from your mouth in words of blame and swells of hate. You label the other person the villain, the bad guy. You attack their character, motives, and actions toward you. In violent, mean, angry words, you attack them for what they did. Yes, it may be true that what occurred was terrible, maybe even hideous, repulsive, or gruesome.

Then what? You withdraw to a place of safety within your mind to replay those tapes again and again. And where does this repetitious action lead? It creates a defeating cycle. Few can emerge from this into the light of true freedom and release from the hurt. What I am saying is that you need to make meaning out of a hurtful circumstance, to forgive the offender for the hurt caused, and to move on to something bigger and better for yourself. In counseling, this is called a turning point. It becomes the defining moment in which you choose to be different. This is what I am suggesting has to happen, and it is definitely a moment of a spiritual awakening.

Here is what I have learned from my counseling experience. You can tell you have arrived in a place of healing, when you can relate your painful story to another person with the same pain, and that person finds freedom from their past wound. In doing so, you also have found freedom. You stop referencing the past hurt as being so painful that you can't go on with living. You stop beginning conversations with the story of the pain left behind. You arrive in a place of healing when you decide to move past being paralyzed with fear that it might happen again. You stop playing the victim. You decide to go on to real living instead of being filled with resentment and vengeance. In fierce determination, you move beyond the martyr's role. In making these choices, you step into becoming a whole person. You make meaning out of the hurt by becoming bigger, better, stronger, and more in tune with others' hurts. You choose to move beyond the cycle of going nowhere, like a gerbil running endlessly on a wheel in its cage. You allow the difficulty to shape you into something more than you would have been before the person hurt you, which is something better because you have grown.

I've also found that hurt-to-healing transitions to be true of counselors, ministers, and professional workers. Many of them begin their practice around a significant loss, hurt, or personal issue in their own lives. In my counseling practice, I've made it a point to observe many of these professionals. I've found that the professional who has made sense out of their own losses or wounds, can use their personal experiences and healing to help their patients with similar wounds or losses. If they haven't made sense of their own losses or hurts, they will not be effective. In fact, God doesn't send people to them for help. Nobody will show up. Even highly degreed counselors, ministers, and social workers cannot keep people in their office. Why? They aren't healers. Their credentials and certifications alone are not enough. Yes, I do believe training is essential, but without experiencing that liberating healing, the professional cannot liberate someone else.

Why? Information does not free people. A professional can share information, but it won't make much of an impact unless the person hearing it is first ready to receive the information, and next believes that the professional knows the path to freedom, based on the professional's own personal history as a victim.

> You, too, will become a healer, and then people will believe you are authentic.

Imagine a counselor trying to coach a parent to get beyond the hurt of the tragic murder of a child, when the counselor has never lost a child. The professional can share truths about getting past hurt, but these truths will be far more effective coming from someone who has lost a child under similar circumstances. Then when strategies for moving beyond the devastating are shared, they will ring with truth and carry an instant value through a mutual bond of hurt and healing. You, too, will become a healer, and then people will believe you are authentic.

On the other hand, some people are healers even before official certification or educational credentialing. I've watched people wait for weeks for an opening in the schedule of individuals who were in the process of getting their education and certification. People already found them to be healers. Though they had not yet achieved their degree or certification, they had made sense out of their hurt, applied forgiveness, and had moved on to become somebody significant. This progression gave them authenticity. It was because of what had happened to them and how they learned from the experience. They faced the hurt instead of hiding from it or trying to get revenge. They forgave the offender for what they did. The professional's own growth helped the patient to move beyond the past hurt and embrace the future. It helped free the patient to stop dragging the past into the present; to stop destroying the present with the fear of repeating the past. Each of those habits prevents the patient from being much good to anybody in the present. No one can be whole carrying around a past wound or future fear. No, hurt and hate will destroy the goal of a life well lived. It will deplete your spiritual life, and keep you from enjoying valuable relationships around you.

When counseling others, I could always tell when my patients were healed, because people began coming to them with their same story. These people just began to show up. Is that amazing? Yes and no. I believe that God started sending others in need of healing because these patients were ready to become healers. These patients had begun to make sense out of the wounds or had gotten answers to the drama they were living. God could now trust them to help heal others with the similar loss.

Genuine, sincere respect is relational. This kind of respect treats another as an equal. Non-relational is thinking you are better than someone else. We call this having a superiority attitude. People with a relational style of superiority must learn and acquire the life skills not to act more important than they are. They need to grow up and stop being the bully in their relationships. Most people who have this problem turn to bullying. They are afraid if they don't bully, they will become the victim. This one-down relationship style makes it difficult to develop others, because the message communicated is that others don't have value. If you have a superiority problem, it is important to keep seeking the life skills to live as an extraordinary individual.

Worse than superiority, is feeling you are beneath another. We call this being inferior. It is hard to show genuine, sincere, respect to others when they act like a doormat. Some of you need to work on your self-esteem skills, or need to focus on becoming interdependent instead of dependent. There is something wrong with your formula of living when you are still at home living off mom and dad at 38. Worse yet is losing everything because you have not curbed your appetites and desires. Dependence is a substitute for being detached from your emotions. You don't allow yourself to feel your feelings. So you turn to some vehicle that helps you feel good. This vehicle serves as a substitute to distract yourself either from exploring your feelings or something you use to avoid your feelings. Isn't it interesting that so often fingers are pointed at drug addicts while forgetting that a huge percent of our world deals with being overweight. Both are the same problem. They just are different vehicles that are used to cope with the anxious feelings you are trying to avoid. Both keep you from being relational.

> Here is the truth: It is in the service to others that truth wealth exists!

How can I find the secret to success when there are so many road signs pointing in different directions?

This is the secret of success with one's self and success with others. It is also the path to true wealth. **Here is the truth: It is in the service**

to others that truth wealth exists. You must gather the skills to help people become more than they would be by themselves Show me someone filled with anger toward their situation or others, and I will show you someone who is financially and emotionally broke. Yes, people like that are quick to label and blame their circumstances or someone else for where they are. By the way, these people also aren't much fun to be around. They get stuck in the hurt and respond with anger, which only causes the hurt to fester more. And you know what? If you are honest with yourself, we all have been there. Yep, been there, done that as the saying goes. What's important is not to get stuck there. Getting stuck will sour you and cause those people you regard as important and valuable to distance them from you.

This attitude is a bit like the person who, when bitten by a rattlesnake, immediately goes after the snake to try to kill it for biting them. How foolish! Is your act of retaliation worth driving the snake's poison throughout your body and possibly dying? Of course not! First, you must deal with the wound, and then you must seek medical treatment. If you don't do this, you are likely to die. Your fear and anger may make it seem natural to go after the snake to chop it up into little tiny pieces. However, it won't do you any good. You will end up losing your life, along with everything you prize.

So, when you are hurt, you must not do what may seem natural and go after those who have hurt you. Instead, you have to train yourself to let it go. Is it easy? Not in the least! You must learn how to discipline your disappointments. It is a skill that most of you don't have. It is easier to blame and blame until everyone no longer wants to be around you. Yes, blame is the oldest excuse humanity uses for explaining away their behaviors or circumstances. Why do we play the blame game? Well, it gives you a guilt-free excuse for not taking responsibility for yourself, your circumstances, and your past. Blaming then immobilizes you. It keeps you from taking chances that will help you learn the life lesson before you—adversity comes to everyone. And you need to learn how to deal with loss so that you can get on with living.

So realize that it is in the nature of the rattlesnake to bite you, and that is what a rattlesnake will do. You may think to yourself that it won't, but this is only foolish thinking. Why? It is the way it is, because it is in the nature of the snake. Don't get caught fooling yourself into thinking that everybody else may have gotten caught, but you won't. When you play around with a rattlesnake, eventually you will get bitten. Such thinking is a trap that will ensnare and destroy you.

If you are reading this and find yourself in the trap of blaming your situation or others, recognize that you are living in the past and robbing yourself of the present. Okay, what in the world does that mean? It means the past has happened. It's over. The only place it lives on is in your mind. If you pull the past into the present moment, you rob yourself of the things that could fill your life now with richness and joy. You crowd the present with yesterday's concerns. Allowing yesterday's hurts to crowd today's living, while leaving little space for new possibilities in your life.

There is a parallel truth with worrying about tomorrow. The greatest tragedy is to allow fear to crowd your life with concerns and events that haven't happened. Such fears will suck the life out of you. This one thing I know as truth and it is self-evident, you will never live to your full potential dragged down by past hurts or robbed by fears of the future. And you will never be an extraordinary individual, let alone lead others. Nope! No way! When your life is filled with contempt and fear, people won't follow the path on which you are attempting to lead them. Learning how to discipline your disappointment is crucial to a life well lived. How? Get the life skills needed to tame blame. Find ways to explain the past and deal with your fears or they will rob you of your full potential. Remember, you can measure whether you are healed from the hurt of the past by the people showing up in your life, who have the same wound or fear and ask for your help. So you see why genuine respect for yourself and others is so important to your spiritual health.

1. Do you have significant hurts in your life? What are they? Write them down in short, bulleted points. Make a plan to get past them.

2. Have you found yourself blaming others for the circumstances or place you find yourself in right now?

3. If you get stuck in your hurt, what will it cost you?

4. How do you truly forgive someone who has deeply hurt you?

5. Do you have any resentment or vengeance issues going on in your life now? If you had the chance, would you get even with the person who hurt you? If so, you are probably stuck in your hurt and definitely have not yet forgiven the person who hurt you.

6. How do you make meaning out of the hurt?

7. How can you tell you are past the hurt?

8. What does it mean to be relational? How can you tell when you are being relational? Hint: You make it about them and not about you. If you feel anxious, you are making it about you and not being relational.

9. Why is acting superior not relational?

10. Why is acting inferior not relational?

11. Why is pulling the past into the present bad for spiritual growth?

12. Why is fear of the future bad for spiritual growth?

13. What is the true test that you are healed of your wound? Is there a rattlesnake that has bitten you? Is your life filled with revenge and the need to hurt the person who hurt you?

14. How is respect for self and the respect for others a reflection of your spiritual value system and it health?

FIFTH: *Watch the use of your language and its impact on others*.	Principle # 5

You do this by finding a balance between being kind and doing the right thing. Now being kind doesn't always have to mean you must act meek. I have had some loving words said to me out of kindness that confronted my behavior and attitude at my very core.

I remember a friend named Chauncie once confronting me. After she listened intently to my stories of "how bad I thought I was having it . . ." she looked me straight in the eyes and with truth and gentleness said, "Brad, you know what your problem is?"

"What's that?"

"You have a need to always be right, and it is hurting your relationships," she said.

Now, I didn't like what she said at the time, but I can mark it as a turning point in my life. Later she was able to help me make huge changes in my life. I call her my guru girl. And she did it in such a non-threatening, straightforward relational way. It is called respect.

Watch your words so that they are not harsh or crude. Sometimes you turn off huge groups of people you could do business with by being harsh or crude. Other times you break the spirit of an important person in your life simply by your tone or the harshness of your words. Also, remember that crude or inappropriate sexual language never opens a door worth entering.

A word picture here can be a pebble or a huge rock. You may think what you say is more like dropping a small pebble on the floor, yet to others hearing it is more like the impact of a huge boulder being dropped on the floor. So watch your words and measure your expressions. You must communicate that you know how to treat a person as someone who is significant and priceless to you.

1. Why is your language so important to being relational? Relational is about being in their world and not about being in yours. It is listening to them and not speaking about yourself, dominating the conversation with your stories, or your experiences.

2. What does it mean to find a balance between being kind and doing the right thing?

3. How does being relational allow for someone to help you see the problem differently?

4. Why is the need to be right so destructive?

5. What is the one piece of evidence that you are stuck? It is called BLAME! It takes away your power and makes you ineffective.

6. Why are harsh and hurtful words destructive to the people who are very important to you?

7. Why is it true that being crude or sexually inappropriate never opens a door worth entering?

8. Why is the use of language so important to your spirituality and having strong relationships surrounding you?

| **SIXTH:** *Be honest with yourself and living in honesty with others.* | Principle # 6 |

You do this by remembering that there is a boomerang effect based upon the principle that what you focus on expands. Being critical toward others will only bring criticism back on you. Blaming others and emphasizing their faults or failures will only make others hypercritical of you in return. So, what you say about others will expand.

If you are positive, it will expand and add to your life as well as to others. If you are negative, it will expand and take away from your life as well as from others. Yes, the same is also true of you. I shouldn't have to say that character assassination is wrong or that slandering another's reputation is wrong. It should be obvious. But we all have times when we have told stories to make the other person look worse than we are. You can never get a positive result from slander or character assassination. It only cheapens the one carrying the tale.

Do you keep your word? A big part of being honest is your ability to keep your word and the contracts you make with others and yourself. Keeping your word is represented in marriage vows, paying off a note to a lender, and following through on a commitment you have given to someone important to you. It is honoring promises to family members to be there when they need you. When you keep your word you experience richness, internally and in relationships, that comes with following through on your commitments to others.

> If you are positive, it will expand and add to your life as well as to others.

One of the ways that I suggest change is first to make a promise you can keep and keep it. It is so simple people stumble over it. If you over promise something to yourself, you won't follow through. Fitness centers see this concept played out annually. They make lots of money from January 2nd through the third week of February. People pay huge fees to start exercising, then they quit in about eight weeks. We call them New Year's resolutions. They last about eight weeks because we over promise to ourselves, which sets us up for failure.

There are two great honesty problems in which I see people failing. The *first* is pretending everything is okay when it is not. This creates a double life for those who participate in its trap. There is the life you present to the world and the one you live on the inside. This inside life is where you hide your true thoughts and feelings from others. You often live there out of the fear of being found out as being empty or worthless. You adopt a pretend life to avoid facing empty feelings or the shame of being found worthless. This is not being selfish. It is about selflessness. It is about the loss of the authentic self, and it is the greatest tragedy of all.

The *second* great honest problem is living without passion. Not all of life is about passion, but I've found that passion is the life flow of your internal spiritual being. It gives power to what is really valuable and important to you. I have talked to hundreds and hundreds of individuals over the course of my career, and here is what I've discovered and come to hold as true: **God has stamped a passion into each one of our lives, uniquely placed to help us contribute positively back to all of the family of humanity.** I've also found that many times that passion was born from a deep hurt or significant loss. This passion is not necessarily there to make you a lot of money or to impact hundreds upon thousands of people, but it might. Money is not evil, but the power it brings can be used for evil. So work on your passion. Make sure you give it a disciplined direction. You may perfect your passion well enough that it makes you a lot of money or creates a greater good for others. At the very least, it will bring you feelings of fulfillment and joy.

> You must choose the right action, in the right direction, for the right reason.

Remember, passion without direction is a lost cause. It is not enough to be passionate about something if you never take a disciplined action to achieve it. Talk is cheap. Passion not only needs disciplined action, but direction as well. Neither is it enough simply to take an action. You must choose the right action, in the right direction, for the right reason. Timing and direction are of the utmost importance!

1. Why is honesty so important to a healthy community?

2. Why is it that being critical of others only brings criticism back on you?

3. Why it is that being positive toward others generates positive waves back to you?

4. Why are character assassination and slandering wrong?

5. What is the measurement of honesty?

6. Why is honesty with one's self on the inside so important when it comes to being honest with others?

7. Why is making a promise to yourself that you can keep so important to lasting change?

8. How does pretending everything is okay create a double life for you?

9. Why is passion important to honesty?

10. How do you discover your passion?

11. Why is disciplined action important to passion?

12. Why is direction important to passion?

SEVENTH: *Be appropriate in your sexual conduct toward others.*	Principle # 7

Being appropriate means finding a balance between your sexual expression and your sexual desire. It is the knowledge that you are a sexual being, with natural desires placed within you by the Creator of all things. Your sexual behavior is to be treated as sacred. Sacred means something for which you show deep honor and respect. It is to know and keep healthy boundaries. It is *not* allowing your expression and desire to migrate toward something perverted. We all know that perversion is terribly wrong. I don't need to talk to you about how it is wrong to victimize or exploit yourself or a second party. Making victims is always wrong. It traps them in the past. They become trapped by your malicious, immoral behavior and painful action you have put upon them.

Molestation is always wrong. Rape is always wrong. Incest is always wrong. Mutilation of self or others is always wrong. Humiliating or degrading another for self-gratification is always wrong. Exploitation is always wrong. It has it roots in greed, which is exploiting someone at the expense of another. Expressing your sexual-self casually with another outside of a deeply sacred commitment is always wrong. Don't be caught in the trap of the promise of fun, excitement, and sexual passion. Instead, beware of its high cost and the deep hurt it will bring to yourself and those who are deeply prized by you. When you break your pledge of faithfulness to others and yourself, you unleash destructive damaging forces of hurt and cruelty. Be one who knows and practices healthy boundaries. Sexual intimacy in healthy boundaries is one of the deepest expressions of honesty. It is the heart and soul of the foundation of the lasting hope for any ongoing healthy society.

Desire is the internal barometer of self-expression toward another adult with whom you wish to mate and be a companion. It can be expressed in the highest form between two loving adults through mutual want and yearning to have children within a committed sacred relationship. It is expressed in the promise of monogamy, deep trust, and loyalty when no one is keeping score. Healthy sexual boundaries create the joy of knowing the other person on a deeply physical intimate and emotional level. This sacred desire is the cornerstone of a strong, lasting marital partnership. It also makes up the foundations of a lasting society.

1. Why is having appropriate sexual conduct toward others so important?

2. How do you find a balance between your sexual expressions and your sexual desires?

3. Why is making someone a victim always wrong?

4. I have listed 7 inappropriate sexual expressions. Why are they inappropriate behaviors?

5.   What can you do if you are a victim or know a victim?

6.   What can you do personally if you are the one participating in victimizing someone?

7.   Why are healthy boundaries so important to balancing your sexual desire and expression?

8.   How is desire the internal barometer of healthy self-expression?

9.   How do you know you have your sexual desire and expression in balance?

Five Landmines That Will Destroy Your Most Vital Relationship

There are really five types of affairs in which infidelity is expressed. The first is called the emotional affair. The second is called conflict avoider affair, the third is called the intimacy avoider affair, the fourth is called the exit affair, and the fifth is the sexual addict. Is a landmine really that destructive? Well, let's read further and see. Then you can make up your own mind for yourself.

Landmine # 1 The Emotional Affair

One boundary violation that becomes a landmine to healthy expressions of your sexual behavior in a relationship is the emotional affair. An emotional affair happens when you put the bulk of your emotional energy into the hands of someone outside of your marriage. It's not that you're not talking with your spouse. It is how you converse. Trading information about the kids, mortgage payments, and the daily errands is not the same as sharing your inner most thinking. The emotional affair comes about when you reserve sharing these valuable and relationship-building personal thoughts with someone outside your marriage.

You may hold back on experiences that are funny to you or discussing something that just happened. Instead, you save it up for the other person. Each of us has a limited amount of emotional energy to spend each day. If you spend it outside the marriage, eventually you will not have enough emotions and genuine love leftover to care for the person inside the marriage. If you continue sharing this deep emotional energy with the person outside of the marriage, one day you will wake up and find that you have little in common with your mate. You may even be bored with your spouse. Though the new relationship may not become physical, you will find yourself on the outside looking in on what once was inside the marriage. The marriage is where you should be investing emotionally in its health and building foundations that make it last.

Getting caught up in an emotional affair is easy, especially in the electronic age in which we live. It begins innocently enough (at least you rationalize that to yourself). It may begin as a flirtatious email that generates another one that takes a step a little too far. You can explain your intent as harmless, but the step has been taken. That door you shouldn't go through has been opened, and going through that door leads to a path toward tragedy. This is not the path for which you were designed. Though peering through the door may never end with you participating in the physical act of infidelity, you are unfaithful nonetheless.

An affair, whether emotional or physical, comes with a price. It can cost you your integrity within your family, with your friends, work associates, and even your clients. The price tag carries an emotional cost as well as a financial cost. You know the stories of people in your communities who have crossed this threshold, only to find a painful drama or disaster on the other side. No one wants to be part of a scandal where people in the community are talking about your stupid behavior. Maybe you are one of those stories. Sometimes the cost runs for generations. It can trap you and your children in a vicious cycle that they live out as adults. So set clear boundaries. I've never met someone who regretted setting a clear boundary. But I have met too many people who live with regrets, because they didn't set them. They also have made others live with regrets, disgrace, and grief.

And I tell you, discipline weighs ounces, while regret weighs tons. Promise to set clear boundaries so that you don't get caught in one of these traps. Refuse to lie to yourself, believing that everybody else has gotten caught here, but you won't. It is a lie because we are humans and can become vulnerable at any point in our lives. Be smart and set clear boundaries.

1. What is an emotional affair?

2. How do you know you are in one?

3. Why does an emotional affair create a secret life?

4. What should you do to get out of an emotional affair?

5. What will happen if you don't?

6. What can you do if you have created a sexual drama in your life that is painfully pulling you down?

7. What will an emotional affair cost you and your children and their children?

Landmine #2
The Conflict Avoider Affair

A second boundary violation that is a landmine to a healthy expression of your sexual behavior in a relationship is the actual act of infidelity. It is expressed in the term of the conflict avoider. It is the couple that has a reoccurring conflict where no solution is achieved. There are usually two solutions offered. One solution is hers and the other is his, but neither is a good solution. Thus, the conflict goes on unresolved only to reoccur again sometime in the future creating the same conflict. What the couple doesn't realize is that they need to put more solutions on the table to resolve the conflict, but they don't do it and the problem only goes unresolved.

In relationships with conflict avoiders, one individual embodies what is called a split-self, where one side of the self is over developed while the other side is under developed. This kind of individual is usually overly rational, while the emotional self is stuck somewhere in the childhood surrounding a painful memory. Since conflict in the relationship never really gets resolved, the split-self partner begins to look elsewhere for relief and emotional connectedness. Since the split-self spouse is emotionally dwarfed, the attention from someone outside the marriage rekindles the emotional side that has been denied. Hence, the excitement of romance and the promise of passion ignite emotions that have been stifled, perhaps for years.

A good example of the over-developed rational-self is expressed in the individual who is super responsible. It is the individual who goes to work every day, pays the bills, helps raise the kids, takes care of the home, and gets involved in the community. It is what is expected, so this individual does it, because they have always been good at being super responsible. In fact, they are often attracted to jobs that pay them well for being so rational. One day the load of being so responsible begins to weigh too much. That is when unresolved reoccurring conflict in the relationship emerges, coupled with the thwarted emotions of a lifetime. All these come together, spinning the split-self into an out-of-control orbit that creates the perfect climate for an affair.

Starved for an emotional connection these people begin to seek out a member of the opposite sex who will listen to their lost emotional self. It is not that these individuals are selfish, but that they are selfless. That there is no true solidly developed self. This other person provides them access to their long-dormant emotions, previously denied by their super responsible self. Hence, the groundwork for an affair is laid.

Conflict avoiders need to know that they can resolve conflict with their companion. It is accomplish by adding more solutions to help work out the problems. They need to identify that there is a mutual agreed-upon outcome: "We both want this problem fixed." The partners never agree to a mutual path, because they can't get cooperation from each other to achieve it. Instead, each one holds to their solution as being the only right one, discounting the other's solution. Conflict avoiders also need to learn how to stop avoiding their emotions, get in touch with their childhood wounds, and express their feelings in a healthy way. Above all, they must learn the skills of cooperation while still paying attention to their own needs and feelings.

The conflict avoider's marriage and family provide the pretense that everything is okay and straight while the affair puts them in touch with their long untended emotions. This imbalance is the reason most conflict avoiders seldom leave the marriage, but continue to participate in a series of sexual affairs.

Through my counseling practice, I have found that information, truth, or even pain does not stop this vicious cycle. You can explore the wounds of your childhood. You can learn to put more solutions on the table to resolve problems within the marriage. Yet true recovery takes more. Real healing is tied to a deeper spiritual awakening within the individual. Unless the split-self individual is willing to explore internal core values and find a life purpose, an internal turning point cannot be created. Without that deep awakening, they will never truly break the cycle of infidelity. Nope! It just goes into a dormant state to await the next serious conflict.

That is why I have included this particular topic in this section. I believe that true healing is intertwined with making and keeping your spiritual-self connected through respect for self as well as respect for others, this is the true expression of being relational. I have found this connection only happens when split-self individuals connect respectfully to God and allow themselves to become a new creation. Through this intentional action, the conflict avoider acknowledges the old split-self and allows God to begin a process of internal spiritual healing. Without this experience through God, the conflict avoider continues previous behavior. Simply knowing the truth does not change someone. However, I have found in my counseling practice that through the Creator of all things, such individuals can change.

When the conflict avoider discovers their true inheritance through an open and honest relationship with God, they then can come to celebrate their true selves and are then free to balance the rational self with the emotional self. This balance then allows the split-self and the subsequent conflict-avoidance-coping cycle to be set aside. When individuals choose this direction, the doors to freedom open to become new people who live in better ways. For the first time they can be free truly to be empowered to find deep lasting joy and fulfillment in their marriage.

1.   What is a conflict avoider affair?

2. What roles in the marriage do conflict avoiders play with each other?

3. What does the term split-self mean?

4. How can you know you are dealing with a split-self spouse in the conflict affair?

5. What can you do if you are the split-self spouse?

6. What is most likely to ignite the affair?

7. Why does the conflict-avoider, split-self-individual seek to find another person of the opposite sex to share their emotions with outside of the marriage?

8. How do conflict avoiders set themselves up for an affair?

9. Why does the split-self stay in the marriage instead of leaving for their lover?

10. What are some real solutions to helping the conflict avoider relationship?

11. What are some real solutions to helping the split-self spouse resolve both the split-self and resolve the conflict?

12. Why is facing the drama openly so important to obtaining healing in the conflict avoider affair? The truth is that you can't change what you don't acknowledge.

13. Why is a double life so easy to justify for the conflict avoider?

14. How does spirituality play an important role in the healing?

> ## *Landmine #3*
> ## *The Intimacy Avoider Affair*

The third inappropriate sexual misconduct landmine is the intimacy avoider. In this marriage involving intimacy avoiders, both spouses resolve their issues by learning to look the other way and pretending that all is well. Each spouse lives with the fantasy that total love is found in someone outside the marriage. This behavior is usually brought on in childhood by a parent sexualizing the child, which blocks normal development of self-esteem and interferes with the ability to relate appropriately to others as an adult. This difficulty creates the trap that is brought on by one parent confiding in the child regarding the other parent's sexual behavior or infidelity. In other cases, it is the expression of incestuous actions toward the child, physical abuse, mental abuse, or abandonment. It leaves the child trapped in the feelings of shame creating the coping behavior they practice in the marriage.

The way to identify the conflict avoider marriage from the intimacy avoider marriage is that both partners in an intimacy avoider marriage are participating in mutual affairs. Anger is the central issue for intimacy-avoiders. Additionally, both spouses have a way of explaining and justifying their affairs while pretending to be riding white horses of purity. Both are masters at pointing out the other partner's faults while not addressing their own inappropriate sexual indiscretion.

Cloaked in the fantasy of sexual intimacy with another outside the marriage, the partners in such a marriage go through everyday life without investing energy into the marriage to resolve it issues. Detached from feeling their emotions, intimacy avoiders create a paradox of pursuing the fantasy of the ideal lover while avoiding cooperation to improve the relationship. All the while, they are oblivious to their own difficulties in sustaining emotional closeness within the marriage. These avoiders use their energy to fight with each other rather than cooperating to achieve something greater together. They invest their energies outside of the marriage in a perpetual search for the ideal lover who will want them and meet all their needs. They perceive the partner inside the marriage doesn't. They are masters at perpetuating the fantasy that the ideal lover will meet and understand all of their deep emotional and intimate needs, because no one else has. The marriage, then, provides the social structure of the pretense, that everything is okay and straight in their world while both partners participate in extramarital affairs.

The underlying issue is how to have a crucial conversation with each other without blaming the other for the reoccurring conflict or failure to meet each other's emotional needs. Getting beyond intimacy avoidance is the willingness to face the anger each uses through withdrawal, labeling, avoiding, attacking, silence, and the need to be right. It is acquiring the skills to understand the other individual rather than trying always to get understood. I have found that trying to get understood at the expenses of the closeness of the relationship is way too high of a price to be paying. The solution is to create a respectful open dialogue where it is safe to talk about the problems. An open dialogue creates trust, and trust helps break the vicious, destructive cycles.

If you find yourself in this vicious cycle, I suggest you seek professional help to outline a new plan to build intimacy. I can tell you it will be worth all the growing you will have to do to achieve it. So I suggest that you start today by making a promise to yourself to find a professional who can help the both of you. If your partner is not willing to go, start by yourself. After all, it is your life, and you deserve to live it to its fullest.

As with other intimacy issues, the core problem is still a spiritual one. Consequently, the solution is grounded in the same spiritual awakening with the Creator of all things. With this comment in mind, make a commitment today to take the first step toward healing. It begins with your own self-examination. It is facing the truth about your own behavior. It is acknowledging that your spiritual-self is but a reflection of your internal being which is not in line with healthy core values and a core purpose leading to lasting importance.

1. What is an intimacy avoider affair?

2. What roles do the intimacy-avoiders' spouses play with each other?

3. How is unresolved anger toward the other spouse one of the two core issues of the intimacy avoider?

4. How is an intimacy-avoider affair different than the conflict-avoider affair?

5. What are the root dilemmas that can cause the behavior of the intimacy avoider?

6. How does the fantasy of the "ideal lover" affect both spouses of the intimacy-avoider affair?

7. Why is cooperation linked to closeness in the intimacy-avoider affair?

8. Why is a crucial conversation with yourself and God so important to the healing of the intimacy-avoider affair couple?

9. Why is spirituality important to healing both spouses in the intimacy-avoider affair?

Landmine #4
The Exit Affair

The fourth inappropriate sexual misconduct landmine is the exit affair. Here the affair is expressed in the message from either spouse as they think about ending the marriage. It is shrouded in the questions: "Can I make it by myself on my own?" "Am I still an attractive and desirable person?" "Can I get my spouse to kick me out?" It is the testing question asked by the straying spouse to their perceived reality. "Is the world really how I see it?" It also can be a guilt-free exit so the straying spouse can leave the marriage without taking responsibility for the inappropriate sexual behavior and the pain caused.

The exit affair also can be expressed in the message of "please help me make it out the door." It shows in the split-self spouse who comes to therapy with the betrayed spouse. The split-self spouse then turns over the emotional care of the betrayed spouse to the counselor. This frees the split-self spouse to exit. It is as though the split-self spouse feels more justified in leaving once the betrayed spouse has some kind of emotional support. When the split-self spouse affair has reached this point, the ending of the marriage is almost inevitable. A marriage of mutual emotional satisfaction is definitely over. Even when the split-self spouse remains in the marriage, they usually continue to be emotionally dependent on the affair and maintain the pretense that the marriage and family are fine. If the spilt-self spouse does end the affair, it is only a matter of time until another one begins. The spilt-self individual has learned to depend on being overly intellectual for interpreting meaning in the world, yet disconnected from their emotions. Since this core problem never gets addressed, it continues unresolved. The truth of the matter; what is really going on, gets expressed in a new affair by the conflict-avoider and the intimacy-avoider who turn to "a new friend" to meet their emotional needs. Unaddressed, these unresolved issues once again fling the straying spouse into another emotional liaison.

Triangle relationships are always a part of the exit affair. This new person, referred to as "my friend," helps the straying spouse transition from the marriage into the new relationship. It should be noted that the third party often is not who the straying spouse ultimately remains with after leaving the marriage. The new friend may be the person who helps create the bridge for the straying spouse finally to leave the marriage, but usually is a poor choice as a new mate. Sadly, the new friend seldom is as desirable as the straying spouse perceives them to be. Mostly it is because the person playing out an affair with a married person is usually as emotional unreliable as the exiting spouse.

And who would really trust someone who has become involved in an affair while married to someone else anyway? The very foundation of trustworthy is being worthy of trust. The affair, by its very nature, erodes at the foundation of trust that is essential to a healthy and lasting companionship within the marriage. To surrender the one is to surrender the other. You cannot have it both ways. You are either worthy of trust or you aren't. Keeping your word is either important to you or it isn't. It is your word that creates the ingredients of trust upon which a lasting relationship is founded. It is the building block of all societies. Without trust a community cannot last. This is why I have included the exit affair in the spiritual area of this book. *Trust is the internal compass set to the True North Principle of character and integrity.* We have already discussed that we can ignore the needle pointing us in the right direction. We can discount its truth. We can choose not to follow its path, but the consequences are fatal. Dismissing the True North Principle and its pathway of character and integrity will mortally wound a life well lived and of lasting importance. You will never find and live an extraordinary life when its foundation is built upon behaviors formed without your full attention to character and integrity. It is too difficult. Instead, your life will be filled with scandal and pain for you and the friends and family you value.

The straying spouse who marries the third party of the affair usually finds that the new marriage lasts only as long as the purpose for which it served—exiting the first marriage. Because the real issues for the conflict-avoider or intimacy-avoider never get addressed, they are carried into the new marriage. The split-self spouses awaken to find the same responsibilities and pain they tried to escape in the first marriage, only their pain and guilt are magnified from the broken relationships. Their pain will continue until they face their core problem and make a plan to deal with it. Consequently, the cheap comes out expensive. The door they thought was an exit only has brought greater discomfort. Avoided problems in the first marriage are only magnified in the second, third, . . . or how ever many relationships are involved on this path of destructive, inappropriate sexual behavior. For these spouses, the cheap comes out very expensive.

Wanderers of this path have a core spiritual problem. Finding the right path is not possible, without first addressing the core spiritual issue. Avoiding by leaving does not solve the problem. Pretending it is solved does not solve the problem. It is facing the truth about one's self and addressing the changes that are needed to create a life well lived that leads to the true answer to this problem.

It is beginning a plan to find and live an extraordinary life that will make a difference. It is allowing the Creator of all things to make you a new thing that brings about the change. It is honestly dealing with your own history. Is it easy? By no means! In order to change the cheap coming out expensive, you must invest the time, energy, and cost of change to make it make a difference.

Otherwise, you are trapped in a cheap, unfulfilled life full of endless blame and hurt that will carry over to the next marriage or to future generations. Now that is a tough price to pay, but it will be assessed! It will be paid. So don't buy into the cheap, because it always comes out expensive. Invest in your future by investing in the truth of your present. It is worth it.

The result will amaze you. So will the person you become by traveling its new path! For the first time, you can come to your senses. You can face the truth about yourself and your behaviors. For the first time, you can claim your godly inheritance as a son or as a daughter of the Living God.

Isn't today the best day to take the first step in a new direction to a new life? You will be glad you did, and so will those who are truly valuable and important to you. Trust me. Your first step starts you on the path toward a liberating and amazing life, one you cannot yet imagine. It will become your life well lived.

1.   What is the message communicated by the straying spouse in an exit affair?

2.   Does an exit affair mean the straying spouse will eventually leave the marriage?

3.   How does the third party play a role in the exit affair?

4.   What role does the third party, "my friend," play in the exit affair?

5.   What is the probability of success in a marriage between the straying spouse and the third party?

6.   How is trust the foundational basis of a successful marriage?

7.   How do integrity and character set the compass of our spirituality? What if they don't?

8. Will you find an extraordinary life without attention to integrity, character, and keeping your word?

9. How does the phrase, "the cheap comes out expensive," refer to the cost of healing from the exit affair?

Landmine #5
The Sexual Addict Affair

The fifth inappropriate sexual misconduct landmine is the sexual addict. Here is the full expression of a true double life, and the message is one of emptiness. The sexual addict is a womanizer or temptress. Sexual addicts seek to fill themselves up and suppress their emotional neediness through "conquests" all in hope of gaining love and acceptance. But like other addicts, the conquest is only a temporary fix and never enough. This affair is about the misuse of power and position.

Although they are adults, sexual addicts are responding to an inner emotionally deprived child. Their background usually is rooted in abuse and a family where the child is sexualized as "Daddy's Girl" or "Mama's Big Boy." It is a family where the child is favored and found to be more loveable than the other parent. This role interferes with the child's normal emotional development. It traps them in the early childhood development stage when the abuse first began. Children in these circumstances develop a pattern either of detachment from their feelings or using extreme levels of emotion to express them. They become extremely mad, bad, sad, glad, or scared. Sexual addictions also can be directly linked to abandonment, incest, molestation, and verbal or physical abuse.

These children grow into adults who usually seek high-profile positions where they can gain power in the public eye. Their private lives are a continuing series of sexual conquests in which the risk of being discovered increases with each new contact. Sexual addicts will continue down this path until their behavior eventually spills out in public, such as in an arrest. Their undermining, out-of-control behavior, once out-in-the-open, leaves their entire world and everything valuable and important in it upside down. The devastation caused is like the aftermath of a catastrophic tsunami.

In this kind of affair, it doesn't matter much who the sexual partners are as long as they display youth and looks. People drawn to the sexual addicts usually have a past history of conflict or abuse, and they are pulled by the position of power the addict has. The sexual addict has a long history of many sexual partners, yet one reoccurring relationship theme: "Please fill me up: I feel so empty on the inside." Of course, nothing soothes the pain or fills the emptiness and like every other addict, the sexual addict is driven to abuse repeatedly. With each new conquest, the sexual addict takes more risk causing them to eventually spiral out of control. Seldom is the sexual addict connected to the individuals with whom they have sex. They usually are so detached and out of control that the fear of arrest or catching a sexually transmitted disease doesn't stop them. Married sexual addicts tend to be male, because a man seldom puts up with a sex-addicted wife. A temptress, however, can be an unmarried third party who wields financial position or power.

This sexually addictive lifestyle flaunts between daring and not caring. Participants in this lifestyle hold the belief that they are above the rules, that they are the ones who make the rules. Their internal motto is: "Catch me if you can." When one of the affairs finally becomes public, which they eventually do, it is front-page news that shocks and stuns the people around the sexual addict. Though a sexual addict admits and apologizes for their behavior rarely are they remorseful or genuinely concerned for the damage they have caused. Often they grow more careless, some almost to the point of being considered insane. They can't stop themselves even when stripped of their prestigious position of power and financial livelihood, or become a victim of a terminal disease brought on by their sexual addiction. One thing for sure, their scandalous behavior distances family and friends, usually because of the fear of guilt by association. Even if the family remains together, the sexual addict only recovers when truly ready to confront the addiction and begin the steps to change.

Sadly enough, the spouse of the philanderer often overlooks the affairs, because the marriage, though nothing more than a shell, brings some comfort. Public knowledge of the philandering brings about a flood of extreme humiliation and pain that creates damage beyond one's imagination. Observers typically speculate that the sexual addict's stoic spouse is either valiantly loyal or just plain stupid. Neither is true. The betrayed spouse usually wants to present a positive image before the world. After all, pretending is what they both do so well.

Remember, the family provides the couple with the pretense of a marriage and the ideal family. This is as deceptive as a ten-mile-wide lake that is only an inch deep. The marriage, like the shallow lake, has no emotional depth, which ultimately enables the out-of-control behavior. The spouse may make excuses for the philandering partner, "He really is such a very good person," or "Deep down he really does love me, so he lied to protect me." The excuses allow the sexual addict's behavior and shell of a marriage to continue, a connection riddled with pain and humiliation. It often takes the public outing finally to destroy the charade of the marriage they have lived.

It takes courage for the spouse, for whatever reason, to end the co-dependent role to which they have grown so accustomed to hiding behind. Admitting the problem brings acknowledgement of the history of the sexual addict's behavior and the spouse's ignorant denial. At that point, there is pressure on both spouses to remain the same. Their roles in the co-dependent masquerade are so familiar. But despite the underlining pain in the marriage lie, facing the truths and making changes are also painful. As a former counselor, I know all too well how ugly and sad an addict's actions and aftermath can be.

Most often, a sexual addict is a person with financial means, such as a business owner, CEO, or corporate executive. It also may be a traveling sales person or your neighbor. The root of the problem lies in the emptiness the sexual addict feels within and how that vast hole gets filled.

As with other types of affairs, it is the emptiness from within that fuels the immoral action. It is a spiritual problem in need of a spiritual healing from the inside out. Yes, the addict must quit seeking sex, but simply knowing that does not necessarily change the addict's behavior.

Sexual addiction is a deeper problem requiring a deeper cure. Its behaviors are the outward expression of a spiritual crisis at the heart and soul of the individual. It is a critical loss of the true self. Rediscovering the authentic self is not about self-centeredness, rather it is a spiritual awakening. It is a process of uncovering multiple and interwoven layers of shame that accumulated over the years of destructive behavior. These layers formed each time the sexual addict avoided personal feelings and desperately sought the unconditional love and acceptance they never had. Only a spiritual awakening with God, the Creator of all things, can make and keep this new creation possible. It is both an event and a process that only need a turning point to begin. If you see yourself in the sexual addict, right now is a good time to make a promise, a first step, to begin today. True healing comes to those who seek a relationship with the Creator of this new being that you will become.

It is also my experience that sexual addicts express themselves through multiple addictions. The presenting addiction is just the tip of the iceberg. Most sexual addicts usually have at least three different addictive expressions, including but not limited to: the abuse of drugs (prescription or illegal), alcohol, sex, gambling, obesity, rage, and spending. It can be a multitude of other things. For most addicts, the greater the risk of the behavior, the more potential for the addict will get hooked. It all stems from a means of coping with accumulated shame.

Sexual addiction is about avoiding a bad feeling or seeking a lost one. It is about turning to a vehicle like sex, drugs, or alcohol in an effort to avoid the pain they are trying to get away from or the emptiness they are trying desperately to fill. Let's use the example of the vehicle of alcohol. The addict will use alcohol to avoid their pain or to seek a lost feeling from which they have become detached. The addict takes a drink. The alcohol will for a short time allow them to forget their pain, to get in touch with their feelings, or to fill up their emptiness. The problem is that the addict's body starts to filter away the affects of the alcohol. This causes the addict to return once again to the alcohol to recover the feelings they are trying to find or to avoid. This in turn causes them to go back sooner for a drink of alcohol which sets up the vicious cycle of abuse that will later trap them in its destructive grip. Each time they drink, the affects of the alcohol have less impact to relieve the pain or emptiness. This results in the addict abusing the alcohol more in an effort to get the same release they are trying to achieve. The problem is that once the addict creates the cycle of abuse there is a greater risk tied to it each time the addict uses the alcohol. The problem is that the alcohol has less and less of a relief affect for them. Hence, the addict gets hooked on the alcohol trying to seek the lost feeling or avoid the bad. The end result is the addict must use huge quantities of the alcohol as they desperately try to avoid the pain or to seek the lost feeling to fill their emptiness. The end result is that they get engulfed in its trap of a false promise of relief. Their behavior is full of shame, and it spins them out of control. The results are life-damaging consequences for them both publicly and privately. Unless they can stop this destructive cycle, they will end up losing everything valuable and important to them in pursuit of things that do not have lasting importance.

It is like the prodigal son in the story told to us by Jesus, the Master Teacher. The addict, like the prodigal son, forfeits all their inheritance and never comes to their senses. They never are able fully to claim being a son or daughter of the Living God. They never fully find the true joy of being one of God's own. They try to earn their right of passage back, while all the time refusing to come to celebrate the rich plan the Father has for them as one of His own dear children.

The hope of your healing is tied directly to your relationship to God. It is a relationship that God wants to have with you. In fact, He already has set into motion the mercy and grace you will need to deal with your shame and begin building a new extraordinary life you and your spouse deserve. The journey begins with your understanding of this relationship. So make a promise to today to get to know and develop a relationship with God. Take the first step toward a new you.

> A relationship to God also means relating to people. God often works through others.

Beginning and change require acknowledging and accepting the truth. Remember, you can't change what you don't acknowledge. Here is the truth part—you must review your past behavior. Really consider all of it, and then take the next step. Write a note of forgiveness to the person inside of you. Apologize for not being supportive through all of the difficult, destructive times of guilt and shame. Assure that valuable person within, as well as your offending adult self that you will be there from now on. Open yourself to God's mercy and grace.

A relationship to God also means relating to people. God often works through others. You must learn new ways to relate. Seek professional help that will support you and help you heal. A team can accomplish more than each teammate going it alone. As a sexual addict, you need people who have the experience and training to help you. It is your life, and you deserve to live it to its fullness. Sometimes getting out of the deadly grip of addiction takes the help of a lot of people who know what to do. They have the knowledge, experience, and know how to get you through the landmines and obstacles ahead. It is important to seek their help. Start now!

1. What creates the problem with the individual that leads to the sexual addict affair? What traits do individuals possess that set them up for sexually addictive behavior?

2. Why is power and status so important to the sexual addict?

3. Why do sexual addicts take increased risks until their behavior spills out publicly?

4. What role does the sexual addict's spouse play in the sexually addictive affair?

5. What finally stops the addict's philandering behavior?

6. Why have I listed healing of the sexual addict in the spiritual area of our being?

7. Why is healing both an event and a process?

8. Why is it wise to seek out professional help to get free of this addictive behavior?

| **EIGHTH:** *The sanctity of life should not be taken lightly.* | Principle # 8 |

You do this by finding a balance between justice and mercy while advocating protection for the weak and the small. You can tell the values and character of a people, a movement, an expression of faith, or a nation by the way it protects the sanctity of life for those involved. Does it treat the sanctity of life with a deep reverence and sacredness? Does it understand the pressing needs of the under-privileged, the impoverished, the sick, the dying, the unborn versus paying attention only to the important and privileged? Does it provide protection from those who would use and abuse this sector? Does a particular movement stand against people who rationalize their actions as right when they are actually filled with bigotry and hatred, while seeking convenience for the few?

Upholding the sanctity of life means that we stand up against the sway of public opinion for voices small, silenced by fear, coercion, or bigotry. It's standing for the underprivileged, uneducated, hungry, poor, or unknown. It is speaking out against hate and violence, which attempt to control the weak and the small. It is speaking up in the face of injustice. It is saying, "This just isn't right."

Recently I had the privilege to visit Birmingham, Alabama. While there, I toured the historic Civil Rights Institute. I walked through the 16th Street Baptist Church where a bomb killed four little girls on Sunday morning September 9, 1963. The deaths of Addie Mae Collins, Denise McNair, Carole Robertson, and Cynthia Wesley marked a shift in the way the United States of America related to its black citizens. This perspective change was brought about through the means of the television media. For the first time in history, people were able to sit in their living rooms and watch firsthand the abuse by the mighty and the strong over the weak and the small. Further perspectives of social change were brought about under the influence of President John F. Kennedy and Attorney General, Robert F. Kennedy. Later, President Lyndon B. Johnson, along with Congress, the House of Representatives, Supreme Court, and the Attorney General's Office acted upon and enforced the privileges of the weak and the small against the bigotry of a nation bent on keeping a segment of its citizens oppressed.

Through the Civil Right Act, a nation rose up and said it would no longer remain silent in the face of prejudice and mistreatment of a segment of its citizens. I walked in silence through the sacred halls of a people who rose up and said they would no longer allow themselves to be treated the way their ancestors had been abused, beaten, jailed, humiliated, and intimated. Those who had been sworn to uphold and protect its people turned dogs and fire hoses on them. It took spotlighting the deaths of some of the cause's leaders like Martin Luther King, Jr. and Malcom X to turn the tide of public opinion in a new direction that had ruthlessly ruled for so many years.

And there I was, standing in silence in the Civil Rights Institute and the church where those four little girls died. I put my hand on the wall in the 16th Street Baptist Church. I was standing on sacred ground. As I read the words spoken by Martin Luther King, Jr., now engraved on the walls of the Civil Rights Institute, tears ran down my face. The pain of a nation bent on abusing its citizens in the ideology of being right at the expense of the weak and the small pierced through me in a new way. Truths I had learned as a young child, such as "All people are created equal" moved me. "We the People" silently and reverently rang out through these hallowed places. Perhaps now those unifying words written for a young nation can bring together the present generation as our first black American has been elected to this country's highest office. We the people have come a long way, yet we still have deep roots of hatred and malice to sever. We the people must not let them grow.

I also have walked through the Holocaust Museum in Washington, D.C., where room after room, wall after wall displayed what happened when a tyrannical and manipulative leader named Adolf Hitler talked his nation into committing hideous atrocities against people not of their ethnic group. Horrors were carried out for want of greed and power. In one area was a window twice the size of a train boxcar that was filled shoes. Each pair stood for someone whose life ended in the gas chambers, simply because of their birth ethnicity. Those shoes represented but a small fraction of the people who suffered and died under this leader's rule of tyranny.

Later, I stood among the vast, endless rows of grave markers signified by a cross or Star of David for the men and women who gave their lives to end this tyranny. They were individuals who lived and died who did not stand silent before injustice, when wrong was put forth as right. It is humbling to be in the midst of these people, even after their deaths. I must remind myself, we must remind one another, not to forget how ugly we can become when we are not spiritually in tune with ourselves and our Creator.

Such ugliness has been carried out throughout the centuries and among many people. There were the actions of the Japanese to the Chinese and people of the Philippines during the Second World War; the genocide by Stalin to the Russians and the satellite nations after the Second World War; Mao Tse-tung to the Chinese people; north to south, in Vietnam, Cambodia, and Korea; the nations of Africa against its people. The list continues and is not limited to times of war. It will always continue, as long as the internal moral compass of character and integrity is not guiding our actions and no one is willing to stand up and give a voice to the weak and the small.

And that voice is more than words. It takes disciplined actions that bring about self-awareness to change acts of hatred and malice. It is getting in touch with the Creator of all things and being in tune with the rights and dignity of humanity. It is a spiritual issue requiring being conscientious of the rights of all of humanity, beginning with the individual and flowing outward into the community. It is the responsibility of each individual to recognize the importance of everyone. And it starts with one's own awakening.

1. Why is protection of the weak and the small the balance between justice and mercy?

2. Why are the values and the character of people measured in how they protect the sacredness of life?

3. Why do we need to set boundaries to protect the underprivileged from being exploited?

4. Why is it wrong to promote what is false under the banner of truth?

5. Why is it important to raise a voice to injustice?

6. Why is a voice not always enough?

7. Is it ever right to advocate justice instead of mercy?

8. Is it right to kill the innocent to make a statement about a perceived misuse of being wronged? Is terrorist bombing an example of this type of thinking?

9. Tell someone today one of your stories about a person who was willing to take a stand against injustice. Perhaps that person is you. Tell your story. How did you do it? Take a moment in silence to remember or be remembered. It is important to remember and too easy to forget.

NINTH:
Learn to be satisfied with where you are as you pursue what you want.

Principle # 9

What? How do you do that? You discipline your longings and desires, balancing them with your passions and purposes. So many of us define ourselves by the things we acquire or accumulate, so much that we may lose sight of ourselves as individuals. We become the role rather than the human. When your identity becomes the role or object on which you have placed a high value, you will feel depressed, lost, and lonely without it. Things never will give you meaning or purpose let alone lasting importance. Anytime you identify with something that has form, it eventually will shift and be no more. That is why it is important to be character-and-integrity-centered. If your centeredness is placed on anything outside of yourself, when it shifts so will your worth. External centering is the basis of low self-esteem.

If you are spouse centered, then your worth is based either on pleasing your spouse or your spouse's opinion of you. If you are family-centered, it or each individual's expectations of you defines you. If you are money centered, having money makes you feel powerful and losing it makes you feel worthless. If you are possession centered, you have an emotional worth attached to an object on which you place value. If the object is lost, stolen, or damaged, then your self-worth disappears with it. If you are pleasure centered, your self-worth revolves around the last party you attended and the next one coming up. The opinion of your friends holds your value. What they think of you is more important than living a life of character and integrity. You live to play and fun is more important than anything else. This person is known to abandon responsibilities, work, and family to get to the next party where they more often than not live with regrets they create for themselves by consuming too much alcohol or drugs. Two friends of mine, Mark and his wife Sandy, told me that all the regrets and embarrassments they live with have something to do with drinking too much alcohol at parties.

Self-worth is not limited to pleasure-related notions. For example, if you are enemy centered, your self-worth is determined by keeping score of wrongs done to you. You become so identified with the wrongs that you are filled with blame and the need for revenge. You get trapped in the hurt and the need to get even. If you are church or career centered, your self-worth comes from that community. If that community's opinion of you changes, your sense of self-worth also changes. That is the plight of being a member of a gang, church, corporation or community organization.

So, you see, you will not find lasting importance when your life is focused on things or the opinions of others. They cannot and will not satisfy. They never bring lasting importance. Lasting importance comes by living a life of integrity and character. It is expressed from the inside out. Without the alignment of this True North Principle in your life, you will struggle with getting and keeping all the golden eggs you deserve and living a life of significance.

So the questions you must ask, "Are you satisfied in your pursuits?" "Do you know what they are and why you are pursuing them?" Let's take a moment to consider some things. Get a pen and paper. Really, get them and take a moment to make a list. Ready?

Number your paper 1 through 40. Now, starting with the phrase "I am," begin filling in each number blank with a term that describes you. Take your time; it may not be easy. When I have done this exercise in my counseling sessions, I am surprised by the difficulty that some people encounter once they pass by number 15. When someone breezes through the list all the way to number 40 or beyond, I ask them to cross off anything listed that is a role, such as a teacher, student, parent, husband or wife. Once you look beyond your roles, you are free to peer into your true self to discover who you are as an individual human being. Sad that many people never get past playing roles, and they never realize what makes them unique.

Did you list a lot of roles? Return to your sheet of paper and list who you are and what makes you tick. Describe you. This list comes from your core of being. Once you tap into your being, you are free to describe the heart and soul of the individual you are. Are you the kind of person who is loving, kind, and honest? Are you funny, daring, silly, or charitable? How about the way you keep your word when you give it. Finish your list and see.

When you or any individual identifies only with playing a role, you risk always losing site of yourself and your worth whenever that role changes, or disappears altogether. An example of this is no longer being a wife or husband. Attaching self-worth to a form that will change is the major cause of depression in our society.

The truth is that you are more than a form or a role. You are not titles you have been assigned or self-designated labels. Neither is it true that you are the positions you have earned. You are not defined by the places you have gone, the people you have known, or the wealth you have accumulated, lost or never had. Attaching self-worth to form cultivates a climate that allows the fear of losing it to occur or opens the door to being lost, lonely, or depressed. Giving into this fear creates anxiety for yourself that robs you of your own sense of internal peace.

Getting past the need to label everything is accomplished by forming a sense of individual purpose, an internal guide from which your talents and abilities flow to an external expression of passion. You become awakened as a spiritual being by becoming conscious or aware of defining yourself in terms of being, rather than of doing or having. God has given all of us natural talents, giftedness, and interests. From these abilities, you can express yourself in the world. When you become aware that you are not a label, object, or role, you then are free to pursue and develop your true spiritual self.

1. Why is it important to tame your longings and desires?

2. Why is playing a role wrong for you?

3. How does playing a role set you up for depression, loneliness, feeling worthless, or unable to find joy in your lives?

4. Why is being integrity and character centered essential to a strong sense of self-worth?

5. I have listed eight errors that can cause you to be centered on things that will lead you in a path to live a life of dissatisfaction. Make a list of as many of these errors as you can. How many represent your thinking? Why would they cause you to have low self-esteem? Why would they bring you dissatisfaction?

6. Okay! Did you take out a piece of paper and number it from 1 to 40. Well, I suggest once again that you do and that you fill in the blanks following "I am . . . ." Come on, this is for your own good.

7. Now go back and remove any roles you have listed. What remains? What does it say about the kind of individual you are?

8. Why does identification with a role not bring lasting importance?

9. Take another piece of paper and make a list such as "I am a person who is," "loving," "kind," or "nice." See how many qualities of your character you can list. Trace out how you give and keep your word.

10. Why does the world seems to want to label or pigeonhole you? How do you find true internal peace when people are only interested in your function to help explain who you are to everyone?

11. What labels do you hold on to so tightly that they keep you from allowing joy into your life?

12. What things are you pursuing that may be costing you your spiritual awakening, a personal relationship, your physical health, or intellectual development? Being aware of the cost is the first step in changing the outcome.

TENTH: *Find or create a state of joy and self-acceptance within yourself.*	Principle # 10

You can find joy and acceptance by being authentic to yourself and your giftedness, by being passionate about a cause greater than yourself. Most people want to be a part of a winning team. Nobody I know likes to stay on the team that always loses. Nope! We all want to be winners.

> Guess What? The good news is that you are a winner.

Guess what? The good news is that you are a winner. You don't realize that because you continuously listen to that condemning voice in your head. The voice talks to you about your past and your future. The voice is the endless talk of your ego, a negative rumbling that tries to pull into the present circumstance and results of the past. This, as I've already told you, crowds out the fullness of being present now. The ego voice also crowds the present with conversations about the future and things over which you have no control. Past or future, either one, will prevent you from being fully present to joys possible right now. You miss the smallest of miracles around you, because you are in ongoing conversations in your head about being someplace other than where you are now. This mindless activity steals your joy and giftedness, as well as your ability to contribute your passions to others and yourself, all of which tie in to your authentic self.

So how do you turn off the voice inside your head and get in touch with the authentic self? Good question. You become aware that you are not the voice. You are the one listening to the voice, but you are not the voice. It is your ego that is speaking. The ego crowds you to feed itself. It is the ego that thrives on situations that tell you that you are right and others are wrong. It is the ego that positions itself with projections of you in the future. The ego plays out what you will say and what you will do. It is driven to occupy your thinking, and it robs you of the time really to be in the moment called now.

The greater question is, "What brings you joy and gladness?" Be careful not to go back to wanting something that you think will fill you up and bring you joy. Joy never comes or last through the possessing of things. Not at all! Things don't bring lasting importance. As soon as you acquire something, you long for something else bigger or better or you have to take care of it.

> True joy allows you to express your giftedness to others. From your giftedness, you will find true passion.

No, true joy comes by being quiet and still in the presence of the Creator of all things. Being fully present means you let go of the endless conversations with yourself about your past mistakes. You let go of endless conversations about your efforts in the future and where they will take you. Joy comes when you are still in the moment to be in tune to God. He speaks in the stillness. He speaks to you when you let go of the ego and the need to be right at the expense of making someone or something else wrong.

True joy allows you to express your giftedness to others. From your giftedness, you will find true passion. Passion will pull you along. Passion is greater than acquiring things, titles, or greatness in the eyes of the world. Consider the humble service of Mother Teresa. By physical appearance alone, you probably would not think she had the attributes to become successful. She was not even five feet tall. She lived among people of poverty, sickness, and a caste rejected by society as unclean and unworthy. She faced insurmountable odds, beyond human endurance and understanding, to serve people she felt God had called her to serve. Yet in this small woman, God delivered a great impact upon the world. The impact was enough to award her the Nobel Peace Prize. In the 20th century, probably no other human has set in motion such a wave of positive influence or established a voice for the weak and small as that of Mother Teresa.

Others, however, are following internal passions to greater causes. I think of Bono, the musician and winner of multiple music awards. Some would say he is an egomaniac. He probably would admit that to himself. But there was one day that Bono and his wife, Alison Stewart, stepped up and it changed their lives and the lives of others. After Bono, and his band U2 participated in Band Aid and Live Aid, he and Alison visited Ethiopia to find out for themselves the severity of Africa's famine. They spent six weeks working at an orphanage. The decided to stay and investigate what was going on and that choice created a turning point in Bono and Alison's lives. Bono is now one of Africa's biggest advocates, helping to voice the need and bring about solutions to the financial and health crises in Africa. He works with passion to put this cause onto the agenda of the world's most powerful people.

Bono created a not-for-profit-company called DATA Agenda modeled after the Marshall Plan, which helped Europeans with debt cancellation and trade incentives to rebuild their economies after the Second World War. Bono championed that the African nations needed similar debt relief so that they could begin to be a part of the world community and solve their own problems. He believed that this debt relief would help them face the financial and health crises that potentially keep them under the tyranny of helpless poverty and its collateral consequences.

According to Bono, he has come to see that negotiating in political back rooms is more fulfilling than singing to a sold-out stadium of fans. He is about the art of the impossible. He is a pragmatic advocate who points out the potential of people getting personally involved. He asks for debt cancellation and new trade incentives to help rebuild Africa's economies. He meets with high-profile people and national leaders to voice Africa's concerns.

Bono has decided to be a part of making a difference. Though amazed at the impossibility of the task before him, he believes that together the nations of the world can achieve something great, something that the next generation will say how proud they are that we got involved.

I think of Oprah Winfrey. She too became awakened to the plight of the people of Africa and the next generation who will take leadership. She decided to get involved. Oprah generates lots of interest. Simply mentioning her name solicits strong emotions in people. I call it the pucker-up or duck response. Rarely are people neutral when it comes to Oprah. They rally behind her and what she stands for or are very skeptical of her and what she does. Regardless, Oprah has chosen to get involved in people's lives and she has a following. From her own pocketbook, she financed and built a Girls Leadership Academy in South Africa. She saw a need and followed a dream to make a difference. Through her influence, girls will find a safe place to learn, be inspired to greatness, and honor their South African heritage.

I also think of an inspiring church leader named Bruce Wilkinson, a gifted writer and public speaker. He founded Walk Thru The Bible Ministries, a leadership institute out of Atlanta, Georgia. But one day, Bruce Wilkinson had a turning point that resulted in mobilization of volunteers to help African's learn how to plant backyard vegetable gardens for orphans and the hungry. He also launched "Beat the Drum for AIDS" a program that informs high school students who live in the largest AIDS-infected cities of the world about the misconceptions regarding AIDS and its prevention. He also brought together more than 15,000 leaders in Uganda and Namibia for a reconciliation conference to help bring about racial healing among white and black Africans. He continues to be involved in changing leadership in the world through his seminars and writing.

> You don't have to be a saint, a rock star, or world acclaimed evangelist to dream big and impact the world on a large scale.

You don't have to be a saint, a rock star, or world acclaimed evangelist to dream big and impact the world on a large scale. We all dream of being a part of something significant, but most of us won't be. We want to be that person who turns on the light for others to be awakened. We want to make a significant difference. We want influence and prestige for our efforts. There is nothing wrong with desiring that, and you need not wait around for that big moment.

The truth is that most of you will impact your worlds in individual, small ways. The good news is, those small ways add up collectively to make a huge difference. Most of you will think your efforts aren't really making much of a difference. Let me remind you that even Mother Teresa questioned her efforts. But what a difference Mother Teresa has made in our world.

1. How do you become an authentic person?

2. How do you become aware of the endless voice of the ego?

3. What will happen to you if you become aware of the ego's influence in your head?

4. How does the ego rob you of the joy of the present moment?

5. How does the ego rob you of your giftedness?

6. How does the ego rob you of your passion?

7. What pain or fear is the ego continuously talking to you about in your head?

8. Why will obtaining "things" never fill up your life with happiness?

9. Why is it that in playing a role you end up abandoning your authentic self?

10. Why is the need to be right and the need to make others wrong the drama of the ego?

11. What is the measurement of true giftedness?

12. Why will this lead us to true passion?

13. I have given you four examples of people who are involved in change. What created their awareness? What called them to action? What will make you aware? What will call you to action?

We have now learned the 10 principles to aligning the spiritual compass of your life. It is the 1st of the 4 Major Life Alignments, which are the keys to the formula of balancing your personal achievement. Now let's move on to the next chapter and look at how to put into place a plan for our physical self as the 2nd Key to the Major Life Alignments.

CHAPTER SIX

Getting Together a Health Plan.	Where Can You Begin So That You Don't Fail?

The *Second* of the **4 Major Life Alignments**
Building a good health plan.

Imagine yourself standing in front of the mirror naked. Don't laugh! You are the one standing there! The question you want to ask yourself is, "What part of your body isn't pleasing to see?" If you are like most people, your eyes will travel immediately to that feature you just can't stand about yourself.

If you are a woman, it might be perceived saddlebags on your hips, cellulite thighs, wrinkles on your face, or stretch marks from giving birth. It may be your hair, nose, breast size, height, eye shape or color, complexion or shape of your face. It also could be that you feel your hands, feet, or body shape is not attractive. You have troubles accepting some physical part of you or several parts! Women especially seem to have a list that goes on and on.

If you are a man, it might be that you want to have Mr. Atlas muscles, but they can't be seen beneath extra weight. It may be that you feel you are long and skinny or not tall enough. Perhaps you think your waistline is too big and you no longer can see your feet. It might be that you think your face is too rough, dry, or pox-marked from adolescent complexion problems. Maybe it is your thinning hairline or that you are prematurely gray. It might be that you think you seem old for your age compared to friends.

Most people standing naked in front of a mirror immediately think to themselves, "I don't like the way I look." This is a typical reaction in our culture and it subtracts from your self-worth. This thinking is driven by the way you assume others see you. It is as though you have this internal measuring stick continually subtracting from your value. Then you feel bad because of how you perceive yourself compared to others.

In many ways, we are too hard on ourselves. On the other hand, some of you have allowed health to slip away to the point it will take a major crisis pounding on you before you finally wake up to how important health is to your personal happiness and well-being. It won't be until a significant life-altering heart attack, stroke, type II diabetes, or joint replacement forces you to deal differently with your health before you pay attention to its value. Until that time, you most often will see your perceived flaws in the mirror and cringe with disapproval or even contempt while doing nothing about it.

In his biography, *The Snowball: Warren Buffet and the Business of Life*, written by Alice Schroeder, Warren Buffett is quoted as saying, "It is what you do right now, today, that determines how your mind and body will operate ten, twenty, and thirty years from now." In a story about a genie and the wishes of a teenager, financial tycoon Buffet likened taking care of your body to taking care of a car.

Buffet admits at age 16 thinking of two things: girls and cars. Not being that good with girls, he decided to concentrate more on cars. As much as he loved cars, had a genie appeared and granted him the choice of any car he wanted, he would have asked, "What's the catch?"

The genie would have said, "This is the last car you are ever going to get in your lifetime." Buffet knowing this condition says, "I would read the manual about five times. I would always keep it garaged. If there were the least little dent or scratch, I'd have it fixed right away because I wouldn't want it rusting. I would baby that car, because it would have to last a lifetime." According to Buffet's analogy, each person is like that car. He said, "If you don't take care of the mind and the body, they'll be a wreck 40 years later, just like the car would be."

So ask yourself the questions, "How many pounds overweight do you think it is okay to be at age 50?" Would you say 10 are okay? What would you say to about 20 or 30? How would you respond to being 40 to 60 pounds overweight at 50? The sad fact is that a large percentage of Americans are more than those numbers over weight right now and aren't even 50 years old!

In the *Chicago Health and Wellness,* August/September edition, 2008 on page 13, they quote the July issue of *Morbidity and Mortality Weekly Report* under the title: "1 in 4 Americans Now Obese." It reveals its 2007 research saying the data shows that "25.6 percent of U.S. adults are obese." It used the body mass index of 30 or above to define obesity.

> Your body is the only one you have. Take care of it as you would something sacred.

> *Would you like to find out a guaranteed secret to weight loss?*

Your body is the only one you have. Take care of it as you would something sacred. When you hold your body sacred, you show honor to it and do not neglect it. Physical health is the second of the 4 Major Life Alignments necessary to achieve balance in your personal world, and to make a positive life-changing impact for you and the world around you.

You cannot have the philosophy that you can drive your body all day and night without proper rest. Neither can you eat everything in sight, drink alcohol in excess, smoke, use drugs, not exercise, or drive yourself to exhaustion. No! Taking care of your body is vital to enjoying your life.

Think back to the story of the Goose and the Golden Eggs. You body is the goose. If you don't take care of the goose, then you risk not getting any more golden eggs. To take care of your "goose," you must concentrate on two specific areas: exercise and a proper diet.

On a recent visit to a popular bookstore, I went to the section on health, where I found two aisles of bookshelves, 20 feet long and five feet high filled with books on weight loss. There were books on low carbohydrate diets, low-fat diets, and fat-free diets; fruit, fish, and chicken diets; protein, vegetarian, and fiber diets; fasting and organic diets; the LA diets, along with long-established diets like Weight Watcher's. The shelves even contained books on surgery diets and water and herb cleansing diets. Though the methods for weight loss varied, each presented a plan promising the reader weight loss if you follow the plan. This is the secret to dieting and weight loss. It is following a plan. Without a plan, you will steadily gain weight until you find yourself in the doctor's office at age 50 watching your doctor put the word obese on your medical chart or face a serious health crisis that hampers your quality of life.

So look again in the mirror and think about your lifestyle. Now answer this question: "Are you maintaining good health practices or is your weight steadily climbing or already out of control and putting your health at risk?"

Perhaps you already have realized that you need to change your habits, but you haven't yet done anything about it, or you've tried, but failed. Well, not making even one small change is a plan for failure, because failure comes about when you don't put into practice a few disciplines each day.

A few failures allowed everyday in your eating and exercising plans eventually add up to many, showing up as obesity or major health problems. At that point, it takes extreme efforts on your part to undo this pattern.

The good news is that you can begin now! Today you can begin to influence your wellness by developing a plan for success by practicing a few daily disciplines. Practiced every day, these daily disciplines will put you on the road to long-term good health. Yes, you can extend your life by years with just a few daily disciplines. Soon you will begin to see remarkable results. You don't have to go at it like a maniac, torturing yourself and making everyone around you miserable while you try to turn around years of neglect. Nope! Success is yours in small steps practiced daily.

This sounds rather easy, doesn't it? You may be wondering then, why do people fail? Because it is just as easy not to take these steps.

It is easy to be lazy; easy to think that it doesn't matter. It is easy to buy bigger clothes. It is easy to ignore the doctor and the test that says you are obese. It is easy to start exercising and dieting, and then quit.

How do I guarantee that I won't fail?

Mostly people fail in their exercise and dieting plans because they over promise. When you over promise, you set yourself up for failure because you make a promise you won't and don't keep. It is just that basic. And that's why diets and exercise programs fail to work. So when you start this next diet and exercise regime, try the reverse of this plan for failure. Make a promise that you know you can keep and then keep it. Build in success by setting steps that you know you can follow. When you over promise, you likely can't keep up the promise and will soon be back on the same path you were before starting the exercise or diet plan. When that happens, your self-esteem gets chipped, because you've broken a promise to yourself. It sets you up for failure and that results in lowering your self-esteem. Overpromising is the first step to failure and a major reason for low self-esteem and depression.

Excuses that make you fail!

Here is my story. I remember the time a doctor of internal medicine wrote "obese" on my annual physical chart. I showed it to my family physician. We both laughed and he said he didn't think I looked obese. Let me warn you not to take advice about obesity from a doctor who is 30 pounds overweight themselves. Rationalizing your weight problem is easy when the evaluating doctor is also overweight. Rationalizing is telling yourself believable lies. And I was good at it. It took me another 10 years to come to grips with my weight before I was ready to do something about it.

Meanwhile, I have a chronic bad back and have had two lower-back surgeries. Due to that problem, I rationalized that exercising would enflame my lower-back and cause muscle spasms. Besides, I hate to sweat. I would leave an air-conditioned house and drive to work in an air-conditioned car. I worked in an air-conditioned office and, at the end of the day, returned to an air-conditioned home in an air-conditioned car.

Get it? I didn't want to work up a sweat, so I adjusted my lifestyle to avoid exerting myself. Then one day my back went out for no apparent reason. A bad back doesn't really need a reason to go out. It just does, at unexpected times. Anyway, I made an appointment with my back surgeon, who recommended that I go to physical therapy. Of course, I drove to the appointment in my air-conditioned car. At the clinic, the physical therapist put me on a treadmill. There I was in my work clothes, the guy who hates to sweat, about to be tested on a treadmill. Next, he gave me a long, flexible rubber bow without a string. I was to hold it in one hand and shake it. In a matter of just a few seconds, I was winded! Ouch. Now what? Well, I concluded that I wasn't going to pay someone to make me walk on a treadmill and shake a rubber bow. So I canceled my next appointment, went down the street, and joined the local YMCA.

Build a sure-proof exercise plan guaranteed to work!

I took along with me a mentor friend of mine named Jim. He asked me if I could do ten sit-ups. Sure! I got down on the floor. It didn't take long to tell by my red face that I hadn't done ten sits-ups in quite a long time. Each morning, however, I dressed in my exercise clothes and drove to the YMCA. I started with walking on the treadmill for one minute at 3 mph. Then I got off the treadmill and did ten sit-ups. Next, I walked over to the chin-up bard and did five chin-ups. I would then go home.

That was my exercise regime five days a week for three months. Then one day, I decided to push the walking to 1 minute 30 seconds at 3 mph, followed by 10 sit-ups and 5 chin-ups. As time progressed, I moved it to an additional 1 minute 30 seconds on the treadmill at 3 mph, followed by 10 more sit-ups and 5 more chin-ups. It took me months to build up to 30 minutes of walking. I gradually bumped 3 miles an hour to 4.5 or just under, the fastest I could walk but not have to jog. Eventually, the sit-ups turned into two sets of 100, followed by back and leg stretches of 100 count sets.

Note that I started with a simple plan. I made a promise to myself that I knew I could keep, and I kept it. Eventually I was able to move the boundaries of the promise and make a new promise to myself. As I expanded the promises, the most amazing thing happened. I found muscles in my legs, arms, shoulders, and waist that I hadn't seen for years! I still remember how good it felt the first time I could go up the stairs two at a time!

Build a diet plan guaranteed to help you lose weight and keep it off!

My diet plan began similarly, committing myself to a plan for 30 days. My plan was prompted by a 95-pound-thinner son-in-law. When I asked this 6'5" former college football player Ken, what he was doing to lose the 95 pounds he said, "It is simple. I just gave up pastas, potatoes, and breads. They come with every meal, and they have carbohydrates that turn into sugar. That is what creates the weight."

Previously, I said to you not to take the advice of someone already overweight. Neither should you follow the advice of someone who lost weight, but put it back on. Instead, follow tips from a success story, someone like Ken. When I heard Ken's plan, I committed myself to the same plan for 30 days. Guess what? I began losing weight. In fact, I lost 50 pounds within about three months. It was amazing. It has been seven years since I had that conversation with Ken. I have maintained the weight loss, and I am still doing the same exercises I've done over the last ten years. You can do it too. The secret is to develop a plan you can follow, and then follow it. Remember, if you over promise, you won't be following your plan in 45 days. Be sure your promise is reasonable and keep it. Now isn't that simple?

As I continued to follow my plan, I took my pants to be altered. One day the tailor said, "Brad, you are going to have to buy some new pants, because I can't take in the seams anymore your pockets are meeting in the back!"

Now I must say this is something much better to hear than a doctor saying you are *obese*. If you are overweight, you have to try this just one time. It makes all the difference!

You may be thinking, "That's a silly plan for losing weight." Okay then! If it doesn't work for you, then find one that does. It is your life and you deserve to live it with a quality of life that good health brings. There are all kinds of plans for you to follow Just don't fail to do one, because you deserve to live your life with a body that is fit and in shape for the journey toward a life well-lived. Don't let your failure to take action rob you of enjoying your life to its fullest. Especially don't be fooled by having a poor plan that causes you not to be around to enjoy the good life you are trying to design for yourself.

Where do I start to build a health plan I can stick with that will last?

For a long-term commitment start out with a question, "If I were to start a diet today without going overboard, where would I start?

What activity would I choose that, with some routine, would have an immediate impact on my health and wellness?"

Figure out your answer and start with that activity. Start slowly to avoid setting yourself up for failure. I recommend that you start simple and lean into it. Yep, lean into it. Begin with one meal, disciplining yourself in a small way that will begin the journey to a healthy body. You will be amazed with the results and how you feel.

Success is following someone who knows the way.

Speaking of amazing, I have a story I want to share. One day at the YMCA, I was exercising beside a friend I'd become acquainted with named Glenn, who looked to me to be about 63 years old. As we discussed the 60th Anniversary of the ending of World War II, Glenn said, "I should have been dead twice from that war." He went on to say, "I was a belly turret gunner in a B-52 and I took a round in the upper leg on D-Day. It should have killed me, but because of the position that I sat as the gunner in the belly of that B-52, my leg stopped the bullet from going straight to my heart. They took me to a field hospital in England to heal. The rest of the crew continued bombing over Germany. None of them returned from their missions." Hence, he said, "I should have died twice."

"How old do you think I look?" he then asked. Telling him he looked to be about 63, Glenn laughed and said, "I was 25 when the war broke out. Now add 60 to that and you'll know how old I am." He grinned. Well, I'm sure that my mouth dropped open in shock. He was walking beside me at 4.5 miles per hour on the treadmill, something he'd been doing since he retired 15 years ago. At that moment, he became my hero, master, and guru guy. What an amazing story! And I've followed in his footsteps to this day.

Take care
to enjoy
each stage
of life.

*So where do you begin so that
you don't fail?*

Before closing this chapter, I think it is important to consider perspective and balance when it comes to body image and achieving a healthy body. The body is not who we are, but how we observe ourselves in the world. This fact can push people to be continuously obsessed with perfecting themselves and trying to look younger. While I believe it is up to you and me to take responsibility for our bodies in eating, drinking, exercising, and sleeping, doing so should not control us. Yes, take care of your body, but remember that the body is not who you are. It is just a form in which the true self of our conscience dwells. Like any living thing in nature, the body ages and will eventually die. One day you will be released from this form to your eternal existence. That is the true self, not the form reflected in a mirror. The truth is that everything eventually dies because no form lasts forever.

Remember that too many people become so identified with the image of which they are, want to be, or who they are not that they block experiencing full joy in their lives. They get caught up in a cycle of hiding the aging process and perfecting themselves, rather than preparing for the natural seasons of the body's aging. Take care to enjoy each stage of life, balancing healthy habits and activities without becoming trapped in a false sense of attachment to your body. Make time for your true self on the inside. Getting caught in a continual fight against natural changes that come with aging robs you of joy where you are. Acceptance is a healthy habit too.

Now, don't think that I'm giving you an excuse to ignore taking care of your body. No! Neglecting your health is a poor plan. Responsible and caring actions for your physical and emotional health enhance the joys available to you in each chapter of your life. Caring for your physical body is part of attending to your internal care, which is the essence of who you are. From within comes your purpose and that is a major component of a balanced and healthy life that is well lived.

Now let's move on to the next chapter of this book by taking a look at the role of mentoring in achieving balance as the next major alignment of the 4 Major Life Alignments. Building relationships as a mentor or being mentored is a crucial piece of the life puzzle moving you toward an exemplary life. Before moving to the next chapter, spend some time reading and jotting down some responses to the following numbered items.

1. Okay, go stand in front of a full-length mirror without clothes. That's right, naked. No, I am not kidding. ☺!

2. What do you dislike about what you see?

3. What do you like about what you see?

4. Now step on the bathroom scale. How many pounds overweight are you? Write it in code, if necessary, so no one can use it against you. What would you like to weigh? Consider your age and height. What is a reasonable weight for you? What area of your body would you like to change first to bring into alignment where you want it to be? Picture yourself in that shape. Visualization is the place to kick off!

5. Next, think about movement. If you were to start an exercise plan today, what activity do you see yourself continuing routinely enough to begin stepping into a process toward

your own good health? You already know what you should be doing. Start there. If you already are doing such an exercise, you have this internal alignment in place!

6. Finally, make a promise that you know you can keep for doing that exercise. Remember not to overdo it. Just a few disciplines practiced every day that you can and will keep lead you on the path to your wellness. So, write down the promise.

7. Now do the same with your eating habits. If you were to start a diet plan today, where would you start without going overboard? Pick a plan that lets you lean into the diet through small promises you know you can keep. How are you taking care of that car the genie has given you?

8. Why is it equally important to give attention to your internal self as to your physical self?

9. Why is it flawed thinking to believe that the inside doesn't matter or that it is professional to separate your personal world from your work performance?

10. Have you been dieting? How is it going? If it is not working, I suggest you change it. Perhaps you need some help from a professional to get it under control. Maybe you need a life coach or exercise trainer to help keep you accountable. If you don't think you can do this because of past failure, I suggest you get into a support group like Weight Watchers or sign up with Jenny Craig. Sometimes you need accountability to achieve the plan you are trying to implement.

11. Where are you on your exercise plan? Is it working to increase your overall health?

12. Isn't today a good day to develop a plan to lead you to a healthy body? Take a moment to commit to a small-step plan for yourself. Start with your promise, the one you can keep and begin aligning to yourself physically. Write your promise down. It is your life and you deserve to enjoy it by living it to its fullest. I encourage you to revisit this section again in 30 days so that you know you have secured long-term success for yourself in your new health and wellness plan. So takeout a calendar and flip it into the next month. Jot down a note to revisit this chapter again in thirty days. You will be amazed at your progress!

CHAPTER SEVEN

<table>
<tr><td>Why is this mentoring thing so important anyway?</td><td>Why Are Relationships So Important To My Lasting Success?</td></tr>
</table>

The *Third* of the **4 Major Life Alignments**
Building strong emotional alignments through friendship and a mentoring relationship.

Think of someone of great importance, someone who, standing before you, would make you feel astonished, perhaps amazed. Who is that person? Why do they command awe from you? What is their quality of character and conduct?

Now consider their reputation. How important is it to this person's admiration or success? How do they protect it? Why do they have your admiration? How do they create influence that makes you and others want to follow in their path? What about this person commands such presence that others are willing to give of their time, talents, and energies to help them achieve even greater things?

Barack Obama commands my respect. He comes to the senior leadership position of the country in dire times, comparable to that of the great depression era. If it were possible, I would like to sit down with him and discuss various issues, gaining his insights, wisdom, and guidance. I would invest time, money, and myself, to be mentored by him. What would you do to be mentored by the person you chose?

When you choose a mentoring relationship, consider the following questions:

1. What would I give to have an hour of my mentor's time every other week?

2. What would I be willing to pay to sit down with my mentor on a monthly basis?

3. With what would I want to have assistance in my personal and professional lives that might help me grow in significance?

4. How could I prepare myself for each visit so that I would be ready to receive guidance, prodding, or even deep, probing questioning into my conduct and character?

5. How could I become so present and transparent that even during brief visits I would be receptive to life-transforming guidance?

6. What greatness would I want stamped on my life that would make a difference to others I encounter on my life's journey?

7. How would my life be different for having taken the time to experience a mentoring relationship?

Finding a mentor who can crucially interact with you.

Perhaps, like me, you chose someone who is not accessible to you as a mentor. Though you still can learn from the actions of the wished-for mentor, finding a mentor who can interact with you is crucial. Because I cannot sit in council with President Obama, I must choose a mentoring relationship with someone more accessible, but who is in a position beyond where I am currently.

I am not speaking of a business model where an assembly of people is grouped together under an assigned leader whose job it is to help facilitate a project to completion, on time, and under budget. Nor am I speaking of a senior person in the company who creates performance reviews for you. No, you need someone outside your direct chain of command. I am speaking of finding someone who will fill the mentoring role I have outlined and forge a course to make mentoring happen in your life.

Realize that your mentor may not always agree with your decisions and, actions, or you of theirs, but a mentor should take the time to listen. At times, a mentor may give reproof, but it should be delivered in courtesy and kindness as a gentle prod to align your internal compass with your outer conduct.

> Your mentor should be someone above you in the leadership circle who has the qualities of leadership, character, and the position you emulate.

Your mentor should be someone above you in the leadership circle who has the qualities of leadership, character, and position you want to emulate. It should be someone whose strength of character challenges you and others to follow their lead. That leadership can be gentle in spirit, yet strong in character. Tony Dungy, former coach of the Indianapolis Colts, is someone who plays that role well. In *Quiet Strength: The Principles, Practices, & Priorities of a Winning Life*, Dungy said, "But winning the Super Bowl is not the ultimate victory. Once again, just to make certain we're on the same page, it's not all about football. It's about the journey—mine—and yours—and the lives we can touch, the legacy we can leave, and the world we can change for better."[1]

---

[1]   Tony Dungy, "*Quiet Strength: The Principles, Practice, & Priorities of a Winning Life*," Carol Stream, Illinois, Tyndale House Publishers, Inc.

In order for you to have this formula right, it is important to find someone who leads through instruction, training, and mentoring. This person should be able to see something unique about you and within you to bring out your best. Thus, your mentor should have enough maturity to understand you better than you understand yourself and help you develop your skills and character, while enhancing your personal development. Above all the person you select should be proud to be your personal mentor.

> Good mentors lead with minimal *authority*.

Good mentors lead with minimal authority, never having to say explicitly that they are in charge. Their leadership styles are driven fundamentally by strong character and integrity. Because high standards guide their leadership, they demonstrate personal responsibility. Their confidence and confidentiality naturally motivate and empower others. Furthermore, good mentors focus mainly on tasks before them. Look for a solution-driven mentor who continually clarifies what is best for you and the organization. They will give clear and quiet explanations. Good mentors usually use a team approach in getting a job accomplished, with a goal of individual improvement for each team member. To attain each job and improvement, they hold you accountable for excellence and expect you to provide your best performance.

You will want to seek a mentor who has influence in their own company and with staff members and customers. Such mentors strive to do the right thing the first time, which is why others value and appreciate them. Though they set high standards, they do not forget the people striving to achieve them. Good mentors are relationship driven.

They are approachable. They give wise counsel in an affirming and nurturing manner. They are good listeners. The best mentors are leaders who teach and coach those around them, especially those that report to them. As such, they look for ways to set you up for success. They deliver quality feedback, giving both praise, and critical assessments. Good mentors facilitate more than they demand.

Now that you know reasons for having a quality mentor, how do you find one? Where do you look and how do you find the right person? Let's start with where you are now. Get a blank piece of paper and draw five to ten circles on it. In each circle, write the name of someone you hang out with on a monthly basis.

Most likely, the people you listed strive for goals and draw a similar income as you do. That's fine for camaraderie, but not necessarily for stretching beyond your current position. Your mentor cannot come from the relationships identified by these circles. You must look beyond these circles. To look in other circles, you must realize where you want to go. You must choose where you want to go. Get clear about the income you want to earn and forge relationships with people at that level. Determine the personal development you want to achieve and seek mentors that will help you get there. You must create a value within yourself that will move you upward. If you don't seek people with a larger capacity of development than yours, you will stay where you are today.

When you look for a mentor, consider these points:

1.   Seek someone in a position you would want to occupy and who is a person of character, integrity, and loyalty.

2.   Look for someone who will help you do it right. I recommend a person who will be open to discussing your answers to the 4 Most Important Questions and someone whose life appears aligned with the 4 Major Life Alignments outlined in this book. Such a mentor will challenge you.

3. See how the person you consider as a mentor handles failure and success. How do they manage diversity? Is this person confident?

4. Mentoring roles work best in a partnership of mutual respect. So look at a potential mentor's ability to handle authority and confidentiality.

5. How does this person direct tasks? How do they deliver instructions and criticisms?

6. Are they open to serving in the role of mentor? Have they mentored anyone before?

7. You and your mentor may need to set guidelines for role expectations and times for discussion.

Will you be able to find all of these mentoring qualities in one person? Perhaps, but probably not. That is why you will gain the most from mentoring relationships when you surround yourself with several mentors. Having more than one mentoring relationship is the secret to successful mentoring experiences.

Being in a mentoring relationship means preparing for the role.

When you are ready to be part of a mentoring relationship, you must be prepared. First, in a mentoring partnership, both the mentor and the mentee must have realistic expectations of each other. A mentoring partnership requires setting clear boundaries, adding crucial conversations, exploring opportunities for growth, keeping things fresh, and building a place of safety where both parties can discuss anything on their minds. For growth to take place, such a relationship should apply some pressure toward meaningful results that have a sense of asset building. Whether you are the mentor or the one being mentored, you must invest time and energy for positive outcomes.

When you enter a mentoring partnership, you need to put together a systematic program of personal and professional development that will give you a fresh perspective and new self-awareness. For that to happen, you must overcome resistance to change and avoid shortsightedness so that you can open up to build character, discover internal competency, and set boundaries for a successful life. If you choose a mentor that you have at some time placed on a pedestal high above you, then you will have to get beyond the awe factor. For healthy expectations and collaboration to occur in this relationship purposed for growth, your admiration and respect must be reasonable. A mentor is a guide who can help you know yourself better. You should come away from a mentorship with the knowledge that you are who you are because, in part, of the person who has influenced you.

> Just as important
> as having a
> mentor
> is
> being a mentor
> to someone else.

Just as important as having a mentor is being a mentor to someone else. When you mentor someone, whether that person chose you or you chose them, that person must be someone you want to assume responsibilities within your company, organization, or community. Taking on these roles helps mentees develop to their fullest potential. When you seek someone to mentor, consider a person who has the character, qualities, and potential leadership skills that would make you proud to be their mentor.

1. What are the realistic expectations you need to set for each other when you become the mentor or engage in a mentoring relationship?

2. What are the boundaries you need to set in the mentoring forum? Why are they necessary for success?

3. How do you build a plan for a successful mentoring relationship? What are the foundational blocks necessary to the plan's long-term success?

4. Recognize that not everyone is ready or willing to be mentored.

5. Be realistic in your commitments to each other as mentor and mentee.

6. Most of all be open to change. Especially be open to shaping and influencing direction. If you can't be open to change, the mentoring roles are doomed from the start.

How do you achieve balance in the relationships of your life?

You cannot achieve a well-lived life without taking care of your emotional needs, especially in your personal interactions with family, friends, and business associates. This is why the emotional area of achieving personal balance asks you to examine the relationships in your life. Who are the people that surround you? Who is there by your choice or design and who is part of "the package"? How do they enhance your life?

Ask yourself several questions. First, who have you allowed into your life? You need not go back to high school or consider every acquaintance over the last 10 years, but think of the people you interact with regularly. Who are the people who influence you most? Think about them and consider this question, "Do these people add or subtract from your value?"

Don't get me wrong; I'm not asking you to determine whether the people you hang around with have intrinsic value. No, everyone has value. What I'm asking is for you to think about how the people surrounding you affect and influence your life. Do you associate with the kind of people who help you develop the best qualities of your character and grow emotionally strong? Does your relationship with them help you develop enhancing life skills? Are they investing in you in a way that can help lead you to a higher place? Consider also whether your closest comrades are the kind of individuals who help you accumulate and hold on to your wealth or possess the strength of character to guide you toward becoming somebody of significance?

If your answers are no, then it's time to look at the relationships in your life and evaluate whether or not you need to limit your associations. That may sound uncaring, but if you continue to hang around people who do not encourage and compel you forward, you will lose track of the passion and purpose of your life. If you don't, they will lead you in another direction. You don't have to cut them out of your life completely, but you might consider limiting your time with them.

Equally important is evaluating the overlapping circles of people around you. Decide who you want to invite into those circles to help you develop into the kind of individual who leaves a significant impact on others' lives. The people you include in these circles are not just friends, family, and business associates, they are also community members from whom you can learn and grow, who can be mentors to you.

In this section, I discuss the importance of including these highly developed individuals in your life. These people will help you develop in your personal growth. They will help you with your professional skills to be ready when the door of opportunity opens before you. Did you know that millionaires hang out with other millionaires? I'm not suggesting that you make becoming a millionaire your goal, only that you need to be around those with similar goals. They will have a different mindset than people without those goals. Let's face it, millionaires think differently than most people.

So ask yourself the question, "How would I develop a millionaire mind so that I can grow large enough to capture the golden eggs I desire and feel I deserve out of life?"

Seek a couple of mentors who have the position and skills you need to lift you onto a higher plain. It's difficult to lift someone higher than you are yourself. To get to a higher level of development, you need people in your life with those higher life skills to get and keep you there. Remember when you invite people into your life that they must be the ones who will be rigorous in asking you the 4 Most Important Questions anybody can ask themselves. Your mentors also should continually stress the importance of keeping the 4 Major Life Alignments in balance.

1. Take out a pen and a piece of paper. Draw 10 circles on the page. Put the names of the people closest to you in the circles. Do you remember the exercise where you put your thumb of your right hand on your heart? Who is that person represented as being the closest to your heart? Now expand the fingers to include other important relationships in your life. Examples might include children, friends, someone in the community, and your church or work associates.

2. Set clear expectations of your role as the mentor. Clarify the time requirements that you expect both of you to invest to maximize the time and attention each of you gives during the one-on-one meetings. Identify the time and place you will meet. Commit to being there. Don't let other commitments or restraints interfere with your time together. Clarify the out-of-meeting expectations for personal development homework.

3. When choosing someone to mentor, look for someone who is ready to be led through instruction, training, and coaching.

4.   The goal of creating a mentoring relationship is to identify areas within yourself you need to strengthen in your personal development. Thus, it becomes important to outline a written plan you can agree to as well as a path to help you achieve these goals.

Note: You could go to my website: *www.drbrad.biz* and click the tab bar for the store. There are two tools there. The first tool is for measuring your leadership style. The second tool is for measuring your leadership effectiveness. I strongly recommend that you order and then take the measuring tool test as part of the first step of entering into a mentoring relationship. It will give you and your mentor or mentee the concrete feedback that will help lay the foundation of future discussions. It will assist you in showcasing your strengths and those things you will need to work on to change yourself.

All the personal development coaches I've ever read or heard em`phasize the importance of working hardest on you, which is not the same as being hard on yourself. Rather you must examine yourself and work to develop the life skills necessary to grow personally and professionally into the kind of person that others want to follow. You need relationships in your life that will enhance your self-esteem and challenge you by continuously stirring your development to a higher level.

Do you spend too much time trying to look good?

Sometimes people get caught up passing time pretending everything is okay when it really isn't. You pretend your kids are fine when they are out of control and you are at your wit's end. Your response to someone asking, "How are you doing?" or "How is the job going?" is always, "Oh fine." In fact, you give the same answer to a like question about your marriage and your health, while all the time you are falling apart on the inside. You walk around like the living dead, pretending everything is okay when it is not. Pretending is a false self. You use it as a mask to hide the underdeveloped self.

Now, I'm not suggesting you tell anyone who will listen all of your life woes. No! Venting just means you are stuck. What I am suggesting is that you need to find a place where you can be truly honest with yourself. You need people who will allow you to be honest about your family, friends, and yourself. They need to be open to allow you to discuss what's going on in your life and the important things that really matter to you.

Sometimes we allow energy-sucking vampires into our lives. These people are the kind of individuals who suck all the life right out of us. They are complainers. They blame everyone and everything for their miserable existence. They are so negative that no one wants to be around them. Be careful to limit your association with these individuals or they will bring you down.

At one point in my life, I made a conscious decision to limit my contact with people who drained my energy. I didn't want their negative thinking to wash over me in huge swells of contempt. I decided life was short, and I wanted to be around people who believed in the best. I wanted people around me who wanted to grow and become something better. I wanted to work with people who wanted to get it. I set clear boundaries to limit myself from being around people who struggled to take action to be better.

Though I believe people can influence others to develop better behaviors and attitudes, energy-sucking vampires must be in the right place and frame of mind to receive help and make changes. As the saying goes, "You can lead a horse to water, but you can't make it drink." The rest of the saying is, "If you are strong enough to hold the horse's head under water, it will eventually take a drink."

Is that the way to help? I decided to limit my time hanging around stubborn people at the watering holes of life complaining about the water. I don't want to waste my time holding their heads under water waiting for them to take a drink against their will. Instead, I made a choice to find and work with people who want to learn. It is much more refreshing and energizing to the human spirit. Besides, when individuals decide to become awakened, they have much more fulfilling experiences than if you or I try to awaken them. You just cannot force enlightenment.

If you choose, you can try to create an awakening.

Otherwise, you will be like the young girl walking through the English countryside meadow one gloriously sunny day. She is singing sacred songs and hymns out loud and reciting Bible verses. In the midst of her magical moment of godliness, she falls down a well. She cries out in vain, to be rescued by anyone who might be near. Swallowing several mouthfuls of water, she goes down for the third time. Suddenly, she has a deep captivating vision of God. She feels His abiding, peaceful presence. Fortunately, someone throws a rope down the well and rescues her. The miracle of this moment amazes her and moves her to want others to experience the same. So, for the rest of her life, she pushes people down the well with the hope that they will find the same vision of God she experienced.

To influence people, you must develop a relationship with them. You listen to their stories and you share yours. Language is the tool that unlocks the heart. It opens the door to really knowing someone and growing personally. As a counselor, it was my job to listen to my client's stories. Additionally, I've disciplined myself to listen to the stories in my personal life. What do your own stories say about you? Personal stories express your life and help the listener understand how you have experienced life so far. A story filled with complaining, for example, indicates that you are stuck in the hurt or struggling with letting go of the past. Complaining always leads to justifying. Justifying leads to labeling and blaming. Blaming is the art of making others look bad so that you don't have to accept the responsibility to do something different. When you blame, you play the role of martyr.

Do you think you might be in that role? Listen to your language. Are you complaining? Do you justify your emotional position as the victim? If you whine about what someone has done to you, then you are playing the blame game. If your story is about a situation that keeps you from moving forward with living, you have taken on a martyr's role. Living in either of these roles keeps you stuck in past hurt. In these roles, you surrender your personal effectiveness. You get stuck in complaining, justifying, and rationalizing why you can't move beyond the perceived injustice. You speak of your loss of power over the situation. You declare your reasons for giving up your personal freedoms. The result is that you become mentally stuck and you lose momentum. You live in the past while robbing yourself of the present energies to live a life well lived.

When I give this workshop, I ask a volunteer to help me. I want to illustrate what it is like to be stuck. I grasp their wrists with my two hands and ask for a little resistance. I then instruct that person to try to break free of my hold. They immediately begin pulling against me. In turn, I resist by pulling back. After a few seconds I then ask, "Are you trying as hard as you can?" Of course, that leads to more pulling and twisting in an effort to break free. The more the participant tries to break free, the more I hold onto their wrists. Finally, I have the volunteer stop pulling. I mention that the decision made to break free by pulling away actually kept them from doing what would have worked immediately. I suggest they could have stomped on my toe or kneed me. "If you even hinted at kneeing me," I say, "I would have released you immediately."

Working within your Circle of Influence.

It is not for the lack of energy that keeps someone from breaking free. Rather, it's not paying attention to doing what would have worked immediately. If you put huge amounts of efforts into something without getting the desired results, you should see a red flag. It means that you probably are not assessing the situation properly. When you put out lots of energy, it means you are working outside of your Circle of Influence. When you work within your Circle of Influence, you will get immediate results.

Individual's Circle of Concern

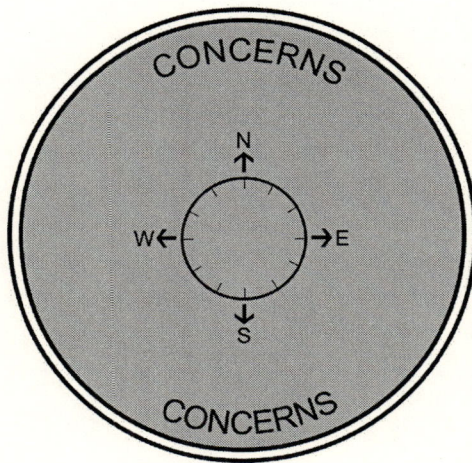

Look at the illustration of the Circle of Influence. Using this illustration or a separate piece of paper, list in the center of the circle where you currently put a lot of energy into managing people or situations. How do you react to them? Those areas probably suck the life out of you. You probably have a lot of blame and complaints. Perhaps you even have labeled someone as the bad guy. Most likely, you have placed the blame on some situation or circumstance. You probably justify it as the reason you have so much difficulty getting rid of or freeing yourself from this problem.

Yet, the path to freedom is simple! Pay attention to your language. Watch for the red flag of exerted effort. Let it be a signal that you are spending too much effort in your language labeling or blaming. Let it represent that you are not doing the one thing that would free you up if you did it immediately. Then commit to doing that one thing. Begin working inside your Circle of Influence. Choose to do the one thing that, when done with repetition, would begin to free you. When you commit to that one thing, you will see the situation begin to change. The path to freedom might not be as drastic as the threat of being kneed in the groin, but it might.

Individual's Circle of Influence

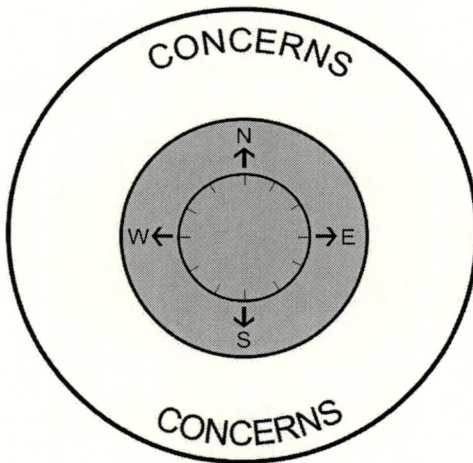

How will you know when you are free? Listen to your language and watch the amount of energy you use to solve a problem in your life. They are red flags to you. When you no longer play the blame game, you are free. When you no longer exert a huge amount of energy to solve a problem in your life, you are free. When you no longer hide behind a false "okay mask", pretending life is fine and it's not, you are on your way to being free. You become free when you become aware of your own language. Your freedom or the lack of it is tied directly to the amount of energy you use *doing the wrong thing for*

the wrong reasons. It is not for the lack of trying, but rather the lack of doing the right thing within your Circle of Influence. Doing the right thing within your Circle of Influence immediately frees you to devote the time, resources, and energy you once used struggling to get unstuck. Now isn't that a new way to look at the problem? How would adopting this new insight help current situations in which you struggle?

How do I include the right kind of people in my life?

One of the biggest roadblocks to having the right people in your life is *the need to be right.* The need to be right gets in the way. It blocks the flow of personal growth while putting barriers between you and others. The need to be right can look like bullying, because when you need to be right, you may become the bully to avoid being the victim. The need to be right leads to being uncooperative. It is not letting go of what you perceive as a flaw in someone else. It is constantly positioning yourself so that you use information against others. When you have to be right, you tend to speak in a scolding tone. You can be harsh and indifferent or even "in-your-face" ugly. The need to be right often makes you hold onto a position when information points out that you are wrong. Most importantly, the need to be right ruins everything valuable and important to you, because you place a higher value on being right than you do on the relationship around you. Moreover, this need comes from a self that is weak and filled with shame.

Be aware of your emotional swell on others!

I want to share a story to emphasize my point. It comes from my days of boating with my family. I used to own a 28-foot, open bow, inboard-outboard SeaRay ski boat. It was designed to carry lots of people, mostly my kids and their friends, and to go fast. At full throttle, it created a wake eight feet deep and sixty feet wide. It is a pretty powerful force of water that would wreak havoc on the shoreline if I didn't slow down in the designated idle zones.

Just as my speedboat created a forceful wake behind it that affected whatever it passed, each of us has an emotional swell that affects others. There are five basic emotions: *mad, bad, glad, sad, and scared.* They drive the reason we tell stories. All of our emotions fall under one of these five categories. Take *scared*, for example. You may not think you get *scared* very often, but you probably do get worried or anxious. You may be uncomfortable using the word *scared*. Nonetheless, you have emotions that fall under the *scared* label, and they affect you and others. Whatever you experience, *mad, bad, glad, sad, or scared*, these five emotions produce the swells you leave behind.

Through various influences, you learned to express these emotional swells in ways appropriate to the surrounding environment. Expectations and pressures from parents, school, and work environments, have shaped your emotional expressions. What you learned to do with your emotions depended on the situation. As a child, you may have been told to be quiet when you were merely expressing happiness or enthusiasm. On other occasions, you may have been shamed when you got frightened or *Scared*. You probably learned to change *Mad* into the more appropriate expression of frustrated or annoyed. If you were *Bad*, you were punished. If that was your experience, then you may have felt that there was no place to express your natural emotions, and you probably learned to detach from or repress your emotions. That is what people tend to do.

When you detach from your emotions, they become bottled up. This will then create an emotional swell that eventually is expressed in inappropriate behavior. Like the wake of a boat moving too fast through an idle zone, your emotional swell creates a wide, threatening, destructive path. You do irreversible things to people you claim to value and love. People who get in your way are damaged. And the broken, destroyed lives crumble around you, because you are not aware of your emotional swell's impact on your most important relationships.

Finding ways to express your emotions in a healthy way is the third area of the 4 Major Life Alignments. Recognizing the important of your emotional swell on others helps you build lasting importance into the relationships you value most. These relationships add meaning to those individuals who influence your world every day. Your well being is dependent upon your building deep, lasting, meaningful friendships. These friendships are the keys to your emotional health. This does not happen by itself. It cannot be left to chance, but is forged by making a plan to have good mentor and mentee relationships to enrich the emotional state of your personal development. This key to emotional health is one of the cornerstones of the 4 Major Life Alignments.

1. Is your need to be right blocking the flow of your personal development?

2. Are you playing the bully or being the victim?

3. Have you placed a higher value on being right than on the health of the important relationships around you?

4. What would those people close to you say about your behavior? Do they feel they matter most to you?

5. What impact is your emotional swell having on others?

6. Have you made a plan to deal with thwarted emotions in your life? It is your life. You don't get a do-over. How is what you do working for you in the area of helping you advance toward a life well lived?

Dr. Bradford A. Seaman

The last of the 4 Major Life Alignments to helping you develop and keep your balance is asking yourself the questions, "How do I develop my millionaire mind? How do I grow large enough to capture the golden eggs I feel I deserve and desire out of life?"

So let's move on to the eighth chapter and the conclusion of this powerful, life-changing book that can lead to a life of true significance.

CHAPTER EIGHT

How Do I
Commit To
Achieve My
Personal
Best By
Developing My
Million-Dollar
Mind?

Could You Be Ignoring The Most Important Tool You Have To Your Success?

The *Fourth* of the **4 Major Life Alignments**
How do I commit to achieve my personal best by developing my million dollar mind?

In the days before the Industrial Revolution influenced the tree harvesting business, lumberjacking was a trade for strong men of physical endurance. One day at breakfast two lumberjacks got into a discussion about their abilities. One had been in the business for more than 30 years, and the other was a strong, young man who was new to the lumberjack trade. Actually, the conversation was mostly the young lumberjack bragging about how many trees he dropped the day before. In fact, as he was taking one of the last bites off his plate, he asserted that he could drop the most trees in a day and knew he would set a new record in the camp.

After listening to the young lumberjack brag on himself, the seasoned lumberjack interrupted the storytelling to challenge the younger lumberjack to a contest. "Tell you what," he said, "I'll bet you that I can drop more trees in one day than you can. Believing that his advantage of youth and strength would make him a sure win, the younger heartedly accepted the challenge.

The next morning both men got up before dawn to begin the contest. The younger lumberjack quickly went to task chopping down trees, using his brute strength to forge his way to anticipated victory. He didn't even stop for lunch or dinner, so that he could take advantage of every hour of daylight possible.

The seasoned lumberjack also got up before dawn to begin the contest with the same successful finish in mind. However, there was one difference in his approach. He stopped every hour on the hour for 10 minutes to sit beneath the shade of one of the trees to be chopped down.

At the end of the day, they counted the trees each man had cut down. The result was that the seasoned lumberjack had dropped ten more trees than the younger lumberjack had.

"How can that be?" the younger lumberjack asked in surprise. "I know you took a 10-minute break every hour throughout the day just to sit in the shade of a tree!"

"Well," The seasoned lumberjack replied, "you are quite right. I did sit under the tree every hour for 10 minutes. And while I did, I also took time to sharpen my ax."

Now years past that era, as well as the Industrial Revolution, the seasoned lumberjack's wisdom still applies. Being successful in the seemingly continuous technological revolution and competitive culture of today's society does not rely on using brute strength and determination. It requires more. Not even cunning ability or a suave appearance will make you successful. More is needed. You must sharpen what may be your greatest tool—your mind.

That is why an *intellectual development plan* is part of the 4 Major Life Alignments and each Alignment is a *key* that unlocks the doors of your success. The *intellectual development plan* is essential because, without one, you will lose the competitive edge necessary to keep you growing in this ever-changing world.

What are you doing to sharpen the ax of your millionaire mind?

You may be countering that statement with some sort of phrase like, "My mind is probably in a slightly lower income bracket." But don't. No matter where you are, you can hone your mind to a sharper focus and intellect with a broader or greater base of knowledge. How do you sharpen your mind? Reading is a good start. What books are you reading? What training are you taking? How are you furthering your education? Do you attend seminars or workshops? Have you set a plan in place to ensure continued intellectual growth? Is it written down? Consider your focus and reaction to that statement. If you have never thought of such a plan, consider the next questions. Are you subscribing to a philosophy of "lumbering" along in life without a clear, precise path to bring about success? Where will that get you?"

Perhaps you are like an high school friend of mine. She stated rather empathically to me one day, "I hate school, especially reading." I made a promise to myself not to read anything after I graduated from high school.

Now that is a poor plan and a bad decision. Adopting this philosophy will surely put her in the category of not taking the time to keep her intellectual development sharp. No! You can't hold onto this kind of thinking and forge a path to success. You won't grow using that kind of thinking.

Maybe you have grown accustomed to coasting through life on your natural skills. Perhaps, you haven't had to apply yourself to make it happen. You may have gotten through school with minimal effort, taken your education as entitlement, rather than something privileged. You have wasted opportunities set before you by allowing mediocrity to be your standard of achievement. You have followed the path of only performing under time pressure to make a push to finish a project. You have convinced yourself, and now are trying to convince others, that you are putting out your best effort. You know you aren't. They know you aren't either.

Ask yourself this question as you observe nature, "*How tall will a tree grow?*" The answer is simple. The tree will grow as tall as it can. Who ever heard of a tree-growing half as tall as it can? So, it should be your goal to grow intellectually at much as you can. We have the most wonderful resources at our disposal. In almost every community there are these institutions called libraries. Each one is filled with a wealth of knowledge and human experience on almost every subject imaginable. Do you know how much it costs to obtain this wealth of knowledge and experience from others? Nothing—that's right, it's free. All you have to do is sign up for a library card. And do you know what? Less than 3% of the population of the United States has a library card. For many people, the library is little more than a landmark when giving others directions. Seldom do they stop in this landmark to tap into its resources. Now what a waste of possible resources that is.

> *What kind of books should you read in your quest to develop your millionaire mind?*

Biographies and Autobiographies

First, consider reading biographies or autobiographies. Learn to search the lives and times of others who have gone before you. Gather from their experiences. Learn from their mistakes. Learn what made them successful. Learn from their failures. Understand the time and circumstances in which they lived. Sometimes reading an individual's story from several different perspectives depicts a clearer picture of what really was going on in the lives and times of that individual. Reading several biographies about the same person is much like sitting in a courtroom where you get to cross-examine different witnesses who participated or watched the same life event. It is fascinating. Make it a habit to include biographies and autobiographies in your library reading.

Books on History and Nonfiction

Second, consider reading books on history. Books on history give insights on people and cultures, helping you understand how they have struggled and grown. History teaches about economics, culture, leadership, tragedy, and triumph. Books on history tell the stories of humanity.

My historical reading list includes books on the generals of World War II, from both the European and Pacific Theater. I've read about the rise to power and eventual fall of Chancellor Adolf Hitler of the Third Reich. I read about the generals who served under him, the ruthless Gestapo, and the Nuremberg Trials and followed World War II battles from Africa to Italy, the D-Day Invasion, and the surrendering of the German forces.

I followed the rise of Lt. Col. Dwight Eisenhower from his days of reporting to General Douglas MacArthur to President of the United States. I read of the Roosevelt years through the Truman administration and Korean War. I followed General Secretary Joseph Stalin, Chairman Mao Tse-Tung, and Emperor Hirohito, the three men who were responsible for a cumulative brutality unmeasured in all of history.

I've read the history of the Civil Rights Movement, the lives of the Kennedys and about the Lyndon Johnson years. I studied the rise and fall of Richard Nixon, and followed the presidents from Gerald Ford through Barack Obama. My reading has included books they have written as well as those written about them.

My World War II reading also included the Pacific battles and the occupation of Japan, which led me to learn about Japan's early expansion into China where the Japanese slaughtered hundreds of thousands of Chinese citizens ten years before Hitler invaded Austria.

My reading has ranged from early history around the world to current wars in Iraq and Afghanistan. The people I learned about on the pages of these books include the slaves Lincoln helped free and the women who worked to free women from social bondage in the Women's Suffrage Movement.

"When the power of love overcomes the love of power, then there will be peace."

Whether or not you are personally interested in history as a topic of reading or for learning historical data, you should include historical books on your reading list for what they can teach you about the human spirit. Unchecked, the human spirit can be cold and calculating, strong and persevering as well as destructive and restorative. The thing history teaches you are that greed and the lust of power needs to be kept in check at all times. This saying is important, *"When the power of love overcomes the love of power, then there will be peace."* (These words have been attributed to people as varied as Jimi Hendrix and William Gladstone.)

Sales and Marketing

Third, you also need some understanding of sales and marketing in your mind-building repertoire. It's helpful to know about the law of supply and demand. You need to understand how goods and services move across an economy. Business and personal success are tied to giving and keeping your word. You need to understand that success is built upon giving the customer or consumer more than what they paid for in goods or services you rendered. Following this practice, you insure that the company or organization you are a part of will thrive even in difficult or economically challenging times or circumstances.

Marketing is the claim of your genuine benefit to the buyer. A sale then delivers on that promise. A good rule of thumb that I try to operate under is to buy when someone else has to sell or shop for the product or service out of season.

I made a lot of money buying and selling houses from people who got into a pinch purchasing or living at the very edge of their income. I also learned not to expand in the harvest time of the business. Why is that important to remember? It is because the harvest always is followed by winter. Some winters can be mild and others are severe. The severe ones can devour all the resources of the harvest. It took me time, and I made some huge mistakes, but I finally learned not to expand during the bounty of the harvest. You can't get stuck in the mindset of thinking the good times will always be there. Nope! The harvest of your efforts can fool you into thinking that making money always will be easy. There have been times that I've lost it all because of the winter that followed an abundant harvest. Set your mind to prepare for the severe winter, so that you can outlast it.

Do you know what I realized? I've found that making large amounts of money takes one set of skills, and keeping money takes an entire different set. Both skill sets are needed. So study and learn a little about sales and marketing to avoid ending up bankrupt and defeated, having to start all over again.

Know what else I learned? I learned that even when a severe winter eats up all your harvest, a spring of opportunity follows right behind the worst winter of loss. What a wonderful place for the Creator of all things to place a season of new opportunity for you to recover. Now remember you can lose everything during a severe winter, yet you still have a millionaire mind when you take the time to learn, learn, and learn some more.

Take, for example, Napoleon Hill. He lost everything he had during the Stock Market crash of 1929, but he gained it all back and more. How did he do that when this great loss happened to him in his late seventies? I believe Napoleon Hill valued his millionaire mind. You see, everything you have accumulated can be taken away from you. If you value your millionaire mind, you can get it all back. So read the books that will open the doors of your thinking. Go to the workshops and seminars to get your millionaire mind enriched. Commit yourself to gather all the necessary tools to help you get there.

How do you create a formula for Investment and Wealth Development?

In addition to sales and marketing, check out books on making wealth and investing. Don't get fooled into thinking your income stream will always last. No! Learn how to create an income stream. Wealth is created by a few daily disciplines practiced routinely.

What does that mean? One way to create wealth is to discipline yourself not to spend all of your paycheck. If you spend all of your paycheck, you will always be broke. I use the 70/30 rule. I've disciplined myself to live on 70% of my income. Now what I do with the other 30% is vastly important.

I use the *first* 10% to give to charity. That is how I get involved in being generous while giving back. I find a cause important to me and I give it 10% of my take-home pay. I research how the organization manages the funds given to it. I want to know whether they are good stewards of the money they raise. Some fund-raising promoters take a huge percent up front. It leaves the organization with very little of the initial money. So do your research before you invest.

The *second* 10% I put into a capital investment fund, investing into something that will increase the capital I have invested. I initially did this through buying and selling cars. I would find a retired person who had taken care of their car. I asked that retiree to let me buy the car when they were in a place of make a trade. I bought the vehicle for $100 dollars more than the dealer would have given them as a trade-in for a newer car. If the car needed repairs, I made them. I then could give my word when I sold the car, guaranteeing it was in excellent shape. I also drove the car, which allowed my car expense to be minimal. I sold the car for a profit, placing that profit from the car back into the capital investment fund. I continued to live my life off the 70% of my earnings, never withdrawing from the capital investment fund to expand my lifestyle.

Eventually there was enough money in the fund to make a purchase of a used house. I found it was always a good decision to buy when someone has to sell. You can always get a better bargain when someone is highly motivated to sell. Whatever the house needed in repairs, I had the financial resources to make them. Again, with the house repaired, I could confidently sell the house, knowing it didn't need work. It was in "ready-to-move-in condition." Eventually resources in that fund grew to the point that I invested in a company, hired a staff, and created a core benefit that was sold nationally. I took the company to a national level eventually winning an award in 2003 for the 9th fastest growing company in that state.

The *third* 10% I put into high-rate mutual funds and bonds. Again, I never touched the investment money to increase my lifestyle. It was placed there to gain value through compound interest. I invested it in others for a return on their efforts. The money yielded is what you will eventually live on in your retirement.

If you are not sure this is a good plan, then come up with one that works for you. But don't get caught without a plan, or you will end up broke and struggling to survive. Nobody wants to finish out the last chapter of life dependent on others for their daily needs.

Networking and Promoting

You are only as strong as the people in the network in which you walk. Networking is surrounding yourself with the kind of people who will ask you the tough questions and challenge you to grow. They will listen to your experiences and give you straightforward answers about what you can do to improve your circumstance, your relationships, and your personal development. As I pointed out in the mentor and mentee section of the third of the 4 Major Life Alignments, you need people who are above you in their personal development and life stage in order for you to grow into the kind of individual people want to follow. You can rise only to the level of people above you.

> Networking is identifying people who will lead you to people in their network.

Networking is identifying people who will lead you to people in their network. You never know who will lead you to the person that will open the door of opportunity for you. You can't afford to get mad at the person in front of you, because you never know whom they might know. Everyone is connected to someone else who is connected to larger groups of other people. In sales, it is common to drive through the first, second, third, and fourth level of contacts before finding the person ready to buy your product or service. Sometimes the opportunities and money don't show up until at least the fourth level of contact.

> Networking is not taking advantage of others by using them to get to others.

For example, Elizabeth, a business associate, introduced me to Kurt who then introduced me to Steven, Jeff, Sally, Robert, Patricia, and Paul. Through workshops, each of these people helped lead me to dozens of others who were searching for jobs and who were in need of my assistance. I wouldn't have met Steven, Jeff, Sally, Robert, Patricia, or Paul if it weren't for Kurt's help. Elizabeth didn't know them, but Kurt did. Each of these people, connected to me through Kurt, opened the door of opportunity for me to present my core message to folks in need through a workshop setting. The money didn't come to me until I was four levels deep in my getting to know people in this network. What would have happened if I had just stopped with my introduction to Elizabeth? Well, I never would have been able to help all the people who showed up at the workshops.

Networking is not taking advantage of others by using them to get to others. No. In fact, it is the opposite. Networking is honoring the person in front of you by honoring the people you meet through that person. You honor these people by providing a core benefit and the genuine features of your product and service. Networking is the most important tool for building your millionaire mind. You can have a wealth of knowledge and experience, but you won't be effective if you don't get it out into the world for people to benefit from it.

Human Understanding

In your pursuit of building your millionaire mind, you need to gather many skills in the area of human development. You don't need to be equivalent to a professional social worker or have a doctorate in psychology to be well versed in understanding how humans think and behave. Yet you can read a wide range of books on these subjects. They will help you understand how to handle and resolve conflict, be aware of your temperament and others', and communicate more effectively. Books in this area can help you parent more effectively, solve problems, increase your leadership skills, develop your spirituality and self-esteem, and improve money management. Read classics from past generations, books on business development, and recent literature on the art of managing people. Without a strong foundation in these areas, your personal effectiveness will waver. Your growth will be stunted, lowering your ability to function well with others. As you gather information for understanding and developing your millionaire mine, be sure you concentrate your efforts in the area of human understanding.

Know something about Legal Matters

You will not be able to conduct yourself in the world for very long without an *understanding of the law*. You do not need to be an expert, but you should know about agreements that you get into when you sign a lease, loan, or contract. Make sure you know what is expected of you and when. Don't assume anything. Read the fine print. It is called fine print for a reason. It is hard to find and hard to understand when you do find it. I recommend consulting an attorney who specializes in the area in which you wish to become involved. An attorney can explain it to you in terms you can understand and help you be aware of considerations not readily apparent. If you are going to pay for the advice, make sure you take it. Remember that old adage: a fool and their money are easily parted. Don't be caught being foolish.

Knowing something about taxes and employee benefits is important. Know what is expected in unemployment benefits laws, workers compensation laws, building and equipment laws, and insurance laws. Ignorance of the law is not a defense that holds up in court.

Some time ago, I was negotiating new space to move my company. It was a larger suite in a different building under another property owner. The owner and I discussed the terms of the agreement and changes to the building I needed to operate my business. We also discussed a cost per square foot. The owner put the results into a *Letter of Intent*. Unfamiliar with this document, I reasoned that because it was not a lease, signing the letter would not hold me to leasing the space. Well, my reasoning was incorrect. A *Letter of Intent* is as binding as a lease. Now I could have gotten mad about feeling suckered into the signing the *Letter of Intent*, but it would have cost me my time and attorney fees to fight it in court. I might have won, but I also might have lost. The reality was that I needed the space for my business to grow, and the document was signed. In the end, I learned a valuable lesson. Before signing a contractual agreement, make sure you understand the document, your obligations, and the consequences of breaking the agreement. It will save you a lot of sleepless nights.

In addition to these recommended areas, it is also important to read books that spark your imagination, lift your spirits, nurture your dreams, and challenge your philosophies. Reading is about opening your mind and more. Reading can develop you as a whole person: it's about learning and expanding possibilities. On the subject of possibilities, are you the kind of person who sees obstacles or solutions?

When you run into difficulties, how do you react? Do you figure out how to handle the problem or do you tend to complain or blame? If you get stuck in the problem by complaining and blaming, it's probably time to realize that you simply haven't grown big enough to handle the problems you are complaining about. Now, don't ask for smaller problems. That's not the solution. Ask to grow bigger so that you can handle the problems in your life. Be the kind of person who searches for the answers. How? Well, start with a logical question: "What can I do to solve this problem?"

What formula do you use when you try to solve a problem?

In the midst of a problem, sometimes you can get stuck in emotions that cloud your vision for finding solutions. Here is a formula I use when first attempting to solve a problem I'm facing.

First I look to my own experience. Have I faced a similar problem in the past? How did I handle that situation? What did I do right? What did I do wrong? Most often, I can solve my problem from my own life experiences without further investigation. I've learned to first try to solve the problem myself before brothering someone else for a solution. It's important to look within for solutions before looking to someone else. Looking within leads to more satisfactory resolutions because you're honoring your values, knowledge, experience, and expectations. That builds your confidence in seeking solutions when you honor your own capabilities.

The *second* step I take is to go to bookstores and libraries for any books related to the problem or situation I've encountered—stories of others who have faced the same or similar problem. Bookstores and libraries are filled with a wealth of human experiences. It isn't necessary to read everything on the topic. You don't need to become an expert before you formulate an action plan. Find five or so books on the subject, or simply browse the table of contents of the books or skim a couple of chapters to grease the problem-solving wheels in your brain. Of course, it may take in-depth research and perhaps a little soul-searching to find solutions to some problems. Before knocking on another's door for advice, do your own homework first.

The *third* step in my problem-solving technique is to check my network of mentors for someone who might help me solve my problem. Seeking outside counsel is the third step, because building my ability to resolve my own difficulties leads to solutions most meaningful to me and strengthens my problem-solving skills. Problem solving with or without the advice of someone else, is a process. It requires you to evaluate the problem, gather solutions, and decide what must be done. No matter how wise and experienced your mentor or advisee is, you are the one who must live with your decision.

Nine essential skills of the millionaire mind

1. *Be observant.* Be the kind of individual who *observes* situations, circumstances, and others. Don't be too quick to jump to conclusions without first being aware of what is going on around you. God gave you two eyes and ears but only one mouth for a reason. Make sure you use the former before the latter. Then reuse them. Often the solution to a problem is within reach; if you just take a little time to *observe* what is going on around you. So tune in and *observe.*

2. *Use reason.* Find the answers to the why questions by reasoning yourself to a conclusion. Before you take action, make sure it is reasonable. Situations that send you into an emotional tailspin usually stabilize when reasoning is applied to the solution. When handling situations, apply logical steps to execute timely and purposeful solutions. Responding from the ego, where emotions rule, usually gets you into deep trouble quickly, exacerbating the original problem. So step back and apply reasoning to the

equation so that you don't fall into the dark deep hole driven by the ego.

3. *Practice visualization.* Be able to visualize solutions. Use your imagination to problem solve before you take action. Picturing solutions is an important step in building your millionaire mind. Visualization lets you see the problem from as many different perspectives as possible before initiating action. Viewing a problem from your own perspective only, gives you a one-sided view. Try to look through another's eyes before forming an opinion and solution. Sometimes the way you have been conditioned to look at a problem actually is the problem.

   When you exercise this practice of visualization, you open new opportunities for different solutions to emerge. Keep looking at the problem the same way, and you will always have the same solutions. Learning to visualize more possible solutions opens your thinking to new ideas, which will lead to endless opportunities for solving the problem.

4. *The Ability to challenge assumptions.* Be willing to test your assumptions to see whether they are valid. Developing your millionaire mind means making sound decisions based upon tested assumptions. Experiment on a small scale before executing the decision fully. A small test of your assumptions allows you to make necessary alignments. It is not wise to draw wide-sweeping conclusions based upon specific, thwarted information you've collected. Logic that goes from specific to general will generally get you into trouble. An example: "The used car I bought was a lemon. All car salespeople are crooked and shady. They are not to be trusted." Flawed logic leads to flawed conclusions.

5. *Face, then act.* Face the *decision* you must make, and then make it! Decide to face the *decision,* and then take the action to

make it happen as you have envisioned it. Deciding is the action step. So many great plans never come to completion, because we fail to take the right action in the right direction to bring about the right results. Now remember, it is not just

> Flawed logic leads to flawed conclusions.

any action. Direction, as discussed in the first chapter of this book is crucial. Consider your direction and develop a plan on how you will carry out that plan. Finally, take action and execute your plan.

Put down some clear, precise measurements so that you know you are being effective and efficient. Nothing is worse than making a lot of noise and getting nothing done. On second thought, there is something worse. It is changing how you measure your plan's success. If you continue to change the measurements, you will never know whether you are being effective and efficient.

6. *Learn from mistakes.* Allow life to teach you from your mistakes. Mistakes make the best teacher, if you let them. Do you fear making mistakes? Sometimes trying to avoid *mistakes* hinders your growth and keeps you from learning! Everyone will make mistakes throughout a lifetime. Some may be costly: others will have minor impact. What's important is to limit repeating those costly mistakes. You can find new ideas and solutions from mistakes. At the least., you can learn not to make the same mistake again.

As long as I'm talking about mistakes, I want to add a related note on "messing up." One of the biggest mistakes you can make is thinking that you won't slip up, even though others have. Right? Are you superior to the rest of the human race? Another lie is letting yourself behave as though the rules and restrictions are for everyone else, but not for you. Along

with that lie is the inflated idea that
you can escape the noose that caught
you previously because you have gotten
smarter. You convince yourself that you
won't get caught again, only to find
your neck in the noose again. Don't go
there. *Learn from your mistakes.* Learn to
keep your distance from those things
that have caused you to fall hard in

> One of the
> biggest mistakes
> you can make
> is thinking that
> you won't slip
> up, even though
> others have.

the dust of regret. Failing to learn can costs you a bundle.
Avoid whatever it is that pulls you into the path of disaster
and scandal. Live lightly, because discipline weights ounces,
while regret weighs tons.

7. *Teach others your skills.* Find people who are asking those
searching questions and seeking solutions, and help them to
grow. Enable them to overcome obstacles in their lives that you
have overcome. *Teach* them to ask the difficult questions. *Teach*
them the understanding and wisdom of applying it. *Teach* them
not to get stuck asking why something happened, but how they
might grow from it. *Teach* them that life requires a plan to make
it unfold before you. *Teach* them that plans don't just happen.
Nope! Plans are well thought out and filled with details. They
are your life's blueprints.

Blueprints for buildings show all the stress points, electrical
connections, as well as the heating and air conditioning ducts.
All of these details are planned out before the first shovel of
dirt is turned. They indicate the mixture of concrete and the
strength of the steel required for the structure's use and longevity.
Well-designed buildings allow for the worst-case scenarios.
The architects provide structural elements that will enable the
building to withstand the worst that nature can hurl at it. Be an
architect in your life and for others. *Teach* those you mentor to
build a plan for the lean times. Such times always happen. When

you plan for them and *teach* others to be prepared, none of you will be completely overwhelmed when they happen. So use your life as an example, and *teach* others how to live a good life worth following.

8. **Reflect.** Understand the importance of *reflection*. Recognize that there are consequences for not taking time to stop and *reflect* on where you have been and how you are going to get where you what to go. Realize the trade offs for not taking time to *reflect*. It's important to understand why things have happened to you in your life, but don't stop there. Take the next step beyond *why* to ask the *how questions*: "How can I get better at what I've failed at so that I don't fail again?" "How can I increase the changes for recurring success in my life on a grander scale?" "How can I team with others who can help me grow?" "How can I draw on the strengths of others so that together we might achieve more?"

Understand that reflecting on *how questions,* increases your capacity to become more. So, if you are going to get caught at something, get caught at being *reflective*. Making *reflection* a habit tunes you into necessary alignments you need to make to keep you on the course to the good life.

To practice *reflection,* you schedule a time for quiet, a place away from your routine and the hustle of life. If you take time to *reflect,* you will walk away in peace. If not, it may be time to plan a get-away to a cabin in the woods or along a stream in the mountains. Perhaps a hotel where you can comfortably retreat from everyday living to read, rest, and reflect on where you are going, how you will get there, why going there is important, and who will be on your team.

9. **Be proactive.** Be the kind of person who sees *solutions versus obstacles.* Someone who looks for solutions captures the opportunities that stem from adversity. Seeing the obstacles for what they are allows

you to stop blaming others and the circumstances around you. It keeps you from focusing on playing the martyr and the victim. If not, you will get stuck trying to convince others how terrible you have it.

Being solution-driven, however, turns your mind into a magnet that pulls you forward, attracting positive outcomes. It seeks cooperation to achieve and obtain more than you would acquire by being competitive.

> Be the kind of person who sees solutions versus obstacles.

Keep in mind the saying of Jim Rohn, a personal development speaker of the 1980's and 1990's as you strive to see solutions as being more important than obstacles. He said, "Work harder on yourself than you do on your job. Work hard on your job and you will make a living. Work hard on yourself and you can make a fortune."

Be connected to something permanent and important.

Happiness is a process, not a place. In developing your millionaire mind, you should be aware of two principles of psychological wealth. The **first principle** is that happiness is more than getting everything you want and desire in life. A perfect set of circumstances in life does not exist. Finding an ideal partner will never happen. You eventually will have health issues. Sooner or later, no matter what you do or don't do your life will end.

Is your happiness tied to money? Wealth is fleeting. And money in itself is never enough to create happiness. When you do gain wealth, it can control you as you try to keep it. Success at work always changes, because the job and environment change. Even if you strive for a happy family, it does not in itself bring happiness. As you develop your millionaire mind, also develop the idea that true happiness is more than a destination. Accept it as a process you must go through to achieve the success. Above all, take the time to stop and smell the roses along the way.

The **second principle** is to understand that happiness is beneficial to helping people function effectively and efficiently in all areas of their lives. Understanding the benefit of cultivating your millionaire mind is the basis to true psychological wealth. Understand that happy people function better at their work, in their important relationships and have better overall health. This is the secret of this book. And it will lead you to a life well lived.

> Now your assignment is to take this book and read it again.

Now your assignment is to take this book and read it again. This time think along the line of how to find and keep this secret by really giving attention to the lessons at the end of each section.

First, ponder them for your own success. Use this secret in your own life and among your own family relationships. Work at being relational with others. Next, use this secret in your business dealings. It is more than being honest. Honesty is important. The 4 Most Important Questions are designed to help you do the right thing for the right reasons in the right direction so that you find and build the life you deserve.

Above all, remember that something I call the Attraction Factor is always at work. If you get stuck in asking yourself the continual question: "*Why is this happening to me?*" You never will fully experience the joys of how the Attraction Factor can bring joy and peace into your life and into your important relationships. To achieve true success through the Attraction Factor ask: "What can I do to make this different?" Using the *How or What Questions* changes the entire universe's energy into helping you achieve what you desire. And don't forget to take action when the ideas begin to flow.

So I personally challenge you to read this book again. Find ways you can use the 4 Most Important Questions you can ask yourself. Tune yourself in on the powerful lessons in personal change by using the 4 Life Alignments. Above all, teach them to others. Teaching them to others help you use them to have a life well lived. So, spread the secret!

1. What activities are you doing to sharpen the ax of your millionaire mind?

2. What commitment must you make to achieve your personal best in developing your millionaire mind?

3. What books are you reading in your quest to develop your millionaire mind?

4. Name the last biography or autobiography you read.

5. Why did you choose that person to read about? What did you learn about them and their era of time that helps you in your present situation?

6. What was the last book you read about history? What did you learn? Why did you pick that era? What answers were you looking for that drew you to that period of history?

7. What was the last book you read on sales and marketing? What did it teach you about how goods and services are moved in the marketplace? What did it teach you about the economy and the cycle of a business?

8. What was the last book you read on technology like Facebook, ITunes, Linkedin, blogging, EBay, or the use of Excel, Microsoft Office, Constant Contact, or building and hosting a website?

9. What was the last book you read on creating wealth for yourself? What formula are you using now that will allow you to retire and not drastically have to adjust your lifestyle? Start now before it is too late. Why? Because you can't offset the lack of daily disciplines that will build your future. You can't goof off in the springtime of opportunity, do nothing in the summer, and then plow and plant like mad in September and get an October crop. No! You have to do the work of each season to acquire the harvest. Determine the harvest and it determines the work of the seasons before it. If you don't have a plan, I bet that I can guess how much money you have in savings.

10. What was the last book you read on the understanding and maximizing your network? Why? It is because it helps promote anything valuable and important to you. Social networking and business networking are powerful tools to help move goods and services through the marketplace. It helps everyone succeed.

11. What was the last book you read on personal development? How about a book on the art of understanding and getting along with others? How about a book on constructively resolving conflict? How about reading a book on the art of having a crucial conversation? How about a book on developing your emotional intellect, your self-esteem, spirituality, or managing people?

12. How about a book on the basics of the law? It could be something as simple as understanding taxes to a corporation. Remember, ignorance of the law is never an argument that will stand up in court.

13. Are you the kind of person who sees solutions or one who blames, labels, and complains about what is happening to you? If you are a blamer, then you are robbing yourself of being present in this moment by crowding today with yesterday's events. They are over. Let them go and make a promise to move on to solve today's problems with today's energies. You can't change the past. It is over. So make a promise to yourself to stop playing the martyr's role.

14. Now take time to name the nine essentials of the millionaire mind. Why are they so important to developing your millionaire mind?

15. Why is connecting to something permanent so important to building an intellectual development plan for yourself?

Above all, recommend this book to someone else. In fact, I recommend you set up a study group. Go through each chapter and set of lessons together. Discuss your answers. You will be surprised at the growth you will experience. So make a promise to yourself and get started!

Get Published, Inc!
Thorofare, NJ 08086
04 February, 2010
BA2010035